BOUQUET OF WHITE ROSES

QUEST FOR TRUTH ABOUT AUNT SUE AND ME

LUCY COSTIGAN

ENLIGHTEN PUBLISHING

DEDICATION

To my family, in love and light:
To those who I share this life with,
To those who have gone before,
To those who will come after.

Bouquet of White Roses:
Quest for Truth about Aunt Sue and Me

Published 2020
By Enlighten Publishing,
14 Thomas Street,
Wexford,
Ireland

www.enlightenpublishing.com

Email: info@enlightenpublishing.com

ISBN: 978-0-9930188-4-8

ACKNOWLEDGEMENTS

Thank you to Niall McGovern for the inspiring critique that has greatly aided my task in making the final version of this book much clearer and, I hope, more enjoyable.

Thanks to Tony Walsh and Theresa Cullen for editing the book and for all their constructive feedback.

Thank you also to Geraldine McGovern for very helpful feedback on the first draft.

Thanks to Anthony Costigan and Sharon Comerford for proof-reading and for sharing their very insightful comments.

Thanks to Michael Cullen of IrishImages.org for the superb book cover.

Thanks to my family for their constant love and support: Tony, Anthony, Theresa, Michael, Paul, Sean, Damien and Hilda, Sharon and Martin, Lisa, Antoinette and Aidan, Kathleen, Val and Yvonne. Thanks to my McGovern cousins: Niall, Patricia, Geraldine, Julian, Rosaleen and Gregory for their friendship and support.

Thanks to Isabel MacMahon, Clara Martin, Maura O'Connor and Carmel Larkin for their much-valued friendship.

In memory of Kila, Lynsey and Sophie Ruby, my wisest teachers and beautiful companions for many happy years.

COVER PHOTOS

AUTHOR'S NOTE

I have written this book to give a detailed account of the unusual situation I found myself in, when, in 1990, I first attended for a spiritual reading. What I was told during that reading had a profound effect on my life, opening me to the possibility that we have all lived previously in other lifetimes and that our lives here are extensions of our spiritual existence. Further studies, investigations, research and travels have all compounded my growing intuition that we each have a purpose, a close circle of souls that we usually reincarnate with, and spirit guides that support us in achieving the goals we have set ourselves in this earth life.

To tell my story authentically, I needed to include personal and biographical information. I also needed to give an account of my family over generations, as they have played a major role in the shaping of my character and my destiny. All events as described here are true, based on my own experiences. I have omitted or changed the names of those who may not wish to be associated with the subject matter of the book.

For any unintentional errors or omissions please notify the publishers so that these may be rectified in future editions.

CONTENTS

ILLUSTRATIONS..12

PROLOGUE..19

INTRODUCTION...23

FAMILY ROOTS, FROM 1904.........................26

BEGINNINGS FROM 1964.............................29

WEXFORD, FROM 1976................................44

DREAMS AND IMAGININGS.....................47

DUBLIN YEARS, FROM 1986........................51

THE READING..56

IF YOU KNEW SUSIE....................................67

PORTMARNOCK GOLF CLUB, FROM 1927.......82

MAKING SENSE OF IT ALL.........................93

WEXFORD AND BEYOND, FROM 1997..........117

FURTHER READINGS.................................122

REGRESSION...128

LIFE AND DEATH...141

IN SEARCH OF TOM....................................153

PORTMARNOCK GOLF CLUB, 2019..............164

ANCESTRAL HEALING................................171

LAYING IT ALL TO REST...........................180

EPILOGUE...186

REFERENCES..191

SONG REFERENCES.....................................193

GLOSSARY...194

FURTHER WORKS BY LUCY COSTIGAN.....203

ILLUSTRATIONS

1. Mike and Kathleen Costigan (née Rossiter), my parents, taken at a dance, Christmas 1950.
2. Mike Costigan with baby Anthony on the old strand in Rosslare Harbour, Co. Wexford with the viaduct and port in the background, 1954.
3. Lucy Costigan aged 7, 1971.
4. Michael Nicholas 'Pop' and Margaret Lucy Costigan (née Flynn) with daughter, Cha McGovern, taken by The Man on the Bridge, Dublin, circa 1938.
5. Lucy Costigan aged 21, 1985.
6. Sue Costigan's birth certificate, General Register Office, Ireland.
7. Portmarnock Club House from postcard, circa 1911, photographer unknown.
8. Portmarnock Golf Club Dining Room, circa 1911, from T.M. Healy's *Portmarnock Golf Club 1894-1994: A Centenary History*.
9. Sue, Tom and Cha in the carpark of Portmarnock Golf Club, circa 1929.
10. Jane Morris née Burden (1839-1914) photographed in 1868 by Robert Parsons (c. 1825-1909), Wikimedia Commons.
11. Sue in the garden of Rosslare Harbour, 1932.
12. The Costigan children in Rosslare Harbour, c. 1920.

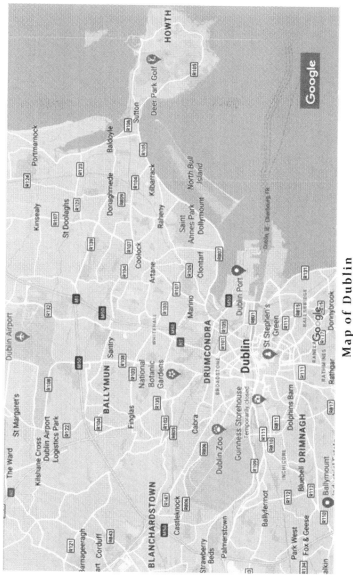

Map of Dublin

PROLOGUE

April, 1931

Sue's throat was healing, though it still hurt when she swallowed. She wouldn't think of that, though. Any minute now, Tom was due to arrive all the way from Dublin. The butterflies played havoc with her stomach. She was so restless she had to keep leaning over to look out the window. The battle-axe of a nurse had just done her rounds so there was no one to scold her. The other patients were finishing lunch, some were praying, others were already asleep, snoring. Her heart went out to the elderly lady with the chronic chest condition who had such trouble breathing.

Sue looked at her watch and wished she could be on her way. She never wanted to spend another day in a hospital, not ever. Wexford Hospital was located on the outskirts of town, a huge rambling building that not very long ago had served as a workhouse. It was austere and devoid of all comfort, the opposite of the Portmarnock Golf Club in Co. Dublin where Sue had been working until the previous month. She tapped her dainty boot against her valise. She was dressed, packed and ready to go. This would be a great surprise for Tom who thought he was only visiting, not taking her home.

Sue took out her mirror, patted her sleek black hair and pinched her wan face. Her blue eyes stared back at her, somewhat lacking their usual sparkle. She pulled her scarf gently around her neck and drank a few sips of water. She'd will herself to be better and put all this behind her. She slipped on her favourite coat with the fur collar, determined to be ready when he arrived. Getting her tonsils out was a drastic step but she only agreed to go along with medical advice when her doctor assured her it would be the end of those bad colds that had left her so ill and drained.

She deliberately switched her thoughts to happier things. There would be the usual dance in the Club at the weekend and just maybe she could go. Imagine if Tom could stay at her home for a few days? Surely that could be arranged. He had planned to stay in town and visit her every day while he was on holidays and she was cooped up in hospital. But all that had changed now. Her mother was a stickler for decorum but just maybe she'd allow him to stay in the guest room. After all, he was her beau and he got on like a house on fire with everyone, especially with Pop and her brother, Mike.

Sue gently drew out the photo of Tom that she always kept with her. He was certainly taller than her, dark and handsome, but he was much more than that. Tom was the bee's knees, kind and loving, a really good sort, with a wicked sense of humour. She had dreamt of meeting such a man. Thank goodness she'd been allowed to work in Portmarnock or she might never have met him.

Thoughts of the first time she'd set eyes on him made her feel woozy. Her first day at work and she was all jittery. Then out of the blue Tom appeared, offering a welcoming handshake, promising to show her the ropes and putting her immediately at ease with his gorgeous smile. From that day she was smitten. All the fun times they'd had in Pormarnock, along with her sister, Cha, brought a deep longing that caught in her throat. She coughed and reached for more water.

She glanced again at her watch. She wondered for the umpteenth time how long it would take Tom to ride his motor bike from Sutton, in Co. Dublin to Wexford Town, a distance of just over one hundred miles. He was always so fast and adventurous but those poor stretches of road would surely slow him down dreadfully. It could take most of the day, she mused. Boy, she couldn't wait to see him, to kiss him and to get going out of this place.

The minutes ticked by interminably. She was beginning to fear that something dire was holding up his journey when suddenly he was there, all hugs and smiles. He couldn't believe it though when she told him she'd been discharged.

"But are you sure you're well enough to travel?" he'd asked, worry creasing his brow. But Sue was having none of it. Her home in Rosslare Harbour might be fourteen miles south of Wexford Town but she was desperate to get on the road, despite her sore throat and the cold wind that was always a feature of the trip. There was no way she'd take the train and miss the chance of wrapping her arms around him, feeling the world rush past and the air zip by, as they flew along the roads at lighting speed.

"If you're sure," he'd given in. "We can take your case down to Mike, if he won't mind taking it home on the train."

Outside, free at last, Sue couldn't wait to hold Tom's hand. Nineteen years old and utterly in love, surely life held in store the fulfilment of all she had ever dreamt. One can only wonder, on that journey home to Rosslare Harbour, with her arms wrapped around her beloved, if Sue glimpsed any portents of the tragedy that was about to unravel?

INTRODUCTION

Tuesday, March 27 1990, 2.30pm

I remember the day well, the day that would prise open my limited understanding of the meaning of life, the day that would pose just as many questions as it answered. I was 26 years old, working as a computer programmer for a now defunct financial institution in Dublin. I may have looked somewhat successful but I was anything but. I was lost in every way that mattered to me: I was in love with a man who still adored his ex-partner; I had no interest whatsoever in the career I had studied years to qualify in; I was sad, confused and lonely, while on the surface trying to keep everything ticking over.

For several years I had been searching to find real purpose. I had told my doctor I was feeling very down and his only solution was to offer anti-depressants. I didn't know what I needed but I instinctively knew it was a much deeper remedy, a salve to lift my wilting spirits. Two friends who I'd met in different circles each recommended that I go for healing to a spiritual centre in Wicklow Street, located in the city centre. At first I was highly sceptical. This could be a 'quack' at work, offering bogus treatments. When my friends continued to tell me of their positive experiences at the healing centre, I decided to give it a go. I was still very cautious as I knew nothing about spirituality, other than the Catholic religion I had been reared in.

On my first visit to the centre I sat in the white leather chair while I received spiritual healing from Brendan O'Callaghan, probably the wisest man I had ever met. Spiritual healing didn't require any form of touch, he assured me, but I could feel the heat coming from Brendan's hands, even when he was standing behind me. I was more than amazed to feel tingling sensations flowing from my head to my feet and waves of energy circling through me, spiralling outwards. I had never felt anything like this before but whatever it was, it had got my full attention. Gone were any misgivings I'd had about Brendan's ability to channel spiritual healing. I was also impressed by his membership of the National Federation of Spiritual Healers (NFSH), based in England.

So, on a cold Tuesday afternoon in March 1990, I was back in Wicklow Street, this time for a spiritual reading. I had no idea what this was, what it entailed or what might happen during it. "It'll be recorded so you can play it back later", Brendan assured me when I rang to book the reading. What I heard that day brought goose pimples out all over my skin and had me hanging on Brendan's every word.

I had always felt something special for my Aunt Sue who had died young from Tuberculosis (TB), many decades before I was born. Sitting in front of Brendan that afternoon, I heard for the first time about past lives, namely I was told that I had lived before in the height of the 1920s. Everything pointed to me having previously lived as my aunt. This revelation might have been interesting and quirky but in this case it fitted me like a hand fits a glove. Since childhood I had felt a deep affinity with the 1920s and I could still recall the joy I felt when first encountering a performance of the Charleston as a schoolgirl. This was the beginning of my quest—through decades of family research, further readings, regression and ancestral healing—to discover everything I could about my Aunt Sue and to unearth our true connection.

FAMILY ROOTS, FROM 1904

I never knew my grandparents as they had all passed on before I was born. My Dad's father, Michael Nicholas Costigan, known as Pop, grew up in Bow Lane, Dublin, in the heart of the Liberties. Pop was known for his congenial disposition and for his love of singing. It was the era of steam engines and his father, Patrick, had been a fitter in the Inchicore Works. Railways in Ireland were an enormous advancement in transport and communications. To become a train driver required many years of apprenticeship, with the coveted position of driver carrying many perks, including the status of officer, increased wages and accommodation provided in a railway house for the duration of service.

Pop was employed by the Great Southern and Western Railway. He worked his way up from cleaner to stoker and then became apprenticed as a locomotive driver. He was promoted to fireman and finally to engine driver. Recently, I asked an aficionado of steam engines what status the position of train driver would have held, back in the early 1900s. I was informed to my amazement that a train driver then would compare, in today's terms, to a jumbo-jet pilot.

The first railway line had been established between Dublin and Cork, a distance of 160 miles, in 1856. Pop was appointed as train driver on this line in the early 1900s and his driving duties frequently led to overnight stays in Cork. Accompanied by his good friend and fellow driver, Joe Deegan, he often called in to the public house, located across the road from the train terminus, at 159 Glanmire Road. The pub was run by Mrs. Flynn and her three daughters, Margaret Lucy, Charlotte and Eileen. A romance soon developed between the eldest girl, Lucy, and Pop. Within six months they were married, on October 27 1904. Joe Deegan married the middle girl, Lottie, the following month.

The Costigans had to move several times during the first years of their marriage, when Pop was transferred from Dublin to Athlone, and then on to Waterford. It had been their wish to set up home in Dublin but, when the railway line was opened in Rosslare Harbour, Pop was asked by the Chief Engineer, Richard Maunsell, to take up a position there, driving the train between Rosslare Harbour and Cork. In 1911 my grandparents finally settled in a very fine railway house in Rosslare Harbour, Co. Wexford. They had six children, Mary Dorothea, known as May; Catherine; Charlotte, called Cha; Susanah, called after her paternal aunt and known as Sue; Michael, my Dad, called Mike; and Joseph, known as Joe. Catherine tragically only lived five months, being found dead in her cot in August 1908.

Throughout my childhood, I heard stories about ancestors who had long passed on. My cousin Raymond, Cha's son, became interested in tracing our family's roots. There was really only one distant relative that stood out for me. My great grandfather, Michael Flynn from Cork, sounded like a real character. He had spent much of his life as a shipwright or ship's carpenter, sailing to exotic locations on large ocean-going vessels in the late nineteenth century. Even when he was married, he let his wife, Charlotte Lucy (née Johnston) run their public house in Cork in his absence. On his return home, he would bring back unusual and tropical souvenirs, such as huge, glistening shells, replicas of sailing ships which he'd made during his voyages, and the greatest of all, a talking parrot with brilliant plumage, called Dick. For many years, Dick continued to arouse curiosity and amusement in the pub in Glanmire Road with his chattering: "Pretty Dick is sick, send for the doctor, quick, quick, quick. Away with the doctor, send for the cook!"

Besides Michael the sailor, the rest of our ancestors seemed to have been hard-working, practical people, rearing their families and keeping a home. None of them particularly stood out. I knew we had some connection with the famous golfer, Joe Carr, through our Dublin relatives. There was of course Susanah, Dad's sister, who had died young. I wasn't told much about her. Over the years, I just heard snippets from my Dad and my aunt May. Sue had been full of life, with so much to live for. Sadly, she had contracted Tuberculosis and had died young, creating a great void in the family. I often thought of her as I was growing up, thinking how tragic it was that she hadn't had the chance to experience a full life.

BEGINNINGS FROM 1964

I grew up in Wexford Town in the 1960s. My parents owned a sweet and grocery shop. They always seemed to be busy, opening up at 8am when the newspapers and milk were delivered, then cleaning counters and containers, refilling jars and cases, calculating if stock needed to be reordered, and serving customers all through the day and long into the evening. Hardly anything came pre-packaged in those days. Biscuits and sweets were kept loose in jars and sold by their weight. Ice creams were cut from the block and then sandwiched between two wafers. Every sale had to be added up, either in your head or written down on paper as we had no cash register. There was so much work involved and there were really busy times when the shop would fill to capacity, especially when the boys from the school across the road ran over at break-time, demanding bags of penny toffees and halfpenny sherbets.

I didn't realise it then but when my three siblings were growing up in the '50s in Rosslare Harbour, about 14 miles South of Wexford Town, there hadn't been a great deal of money and things had been fairly tight. I was much younger than any of them, 11 years younger than Theresa, 10 years junior to Anthony and there were 9 years between my adopted brother, Val, and me.

There is quite a tale to tell about how Val came into the family. Mammy had had two miscarriages and a stillbirth that left her bereft and yearning for a child. She answered an advert from St. Joseph's Orphanage in Kilkenny that asked families to take a boy for the summer holidays. One boy had been picked to holiday with the Costigans but at the last minute he cried and kicked up a stir. The story goes that the Reverend Mother said, "I know who'll go– Val". And so Val, aged 4, was dressed in the new clothes formerly worn by the reluctant boy and packed off to Rosslare Harbour for the holidays. Val returned for another holiday the following summer and began calling his hosts his Mammy and Daddy. He was adopted into the family in 1961. That was the year my dad was made redundant from the Co-Op and my parents decided to open their own store, and move into Wexford Town.

On Sunday, February 9 1964, at three minutes past midnight, I arrived into the family. I was a big shock to my sister and brothers because Mammy had been too afraid of losing me to tell them she was pregnant. On doctor's orders, she had taken to her bed for six months before I was born, having injections and being warned to do nothing but rest. So she took to reading, everything from *Gone with the Wind* to *Wuthering Heights*. Anyway, all that rest did the trick and when I arrived I certainly was a bonny baby, weighing in at over nine pounds.

The first three years of my life were full of happiness. I loved my family and felt deeply loved. My siblings tell me I had much greater freedom than they ever had and I remember laughing and playing on endless summer days in our big back garden in Barrack Street. Mammy read me stories and listened attentively to all the imaginary characters I invented, both human and animal. When my parents had to give-up the shop they had been renting at the Boker, they bought a house with a shop attached just up the road. We moved in before Christmas 1967. The lady who was selling the house gave me a big golden-brown teddy bear the day we arrived. It was such a lovely thought. Sadly though, one of my teddy's eyes fell out and had to be sown back in. He always had a tiny scar but it didn't matter, he was still my favourite.

I went everywhere with Val as he delivered newspapers, potatoes and coal to customers. I remember one sunny morning in 1968 when we walked to the North Station to collect the Sunday papers. Val told me that Robert Kennedy had been shot. The Quay was so still and the sun was warm and glistening as we walked back home, with Val pulling his trolley and I walking beside him. I had a sense of sadness though that something very bad had happened. I never forgot that morning, its beauty and its sadness.

Then there was Anthony who filled my days with such fun, drawing horses and painting ships, making figures and miniature furniture out of plasticine. The house was full of music, TV and talk of films, the Beatles and James Bond, Clint Eastwood and *Man from Uncle.* Theresa helped my dad in the shop. I remember her combing her long dark hair; wearing short dresses and long white boots. I wanted to be grown up like her. She married Sean Cullen when I

31

was eight and I missed her a lot, even though she still lived in town.

Everything had been so great before I started school. From day one I hated school, hated the rules, the social pecking order, the judgements, the cross way in which the nuns and teachers often spoke, the jeers of other children, the threat of punishment, the feeling that I wasn't right and could never be enough. Those feelings filtered into my core and dampened down my joyous spirit. I have tried to erase them and in some ways I have succeeded, but a residue remains.

I remember learning to write my name. I used to put the 'y' backwards. I loved my name although for the first few years I'm told I called myself Lighty. Later, when I noticed that women changed their surnames when they got married, I told my parents that I'd never change mine. I felt my name was perfect for me.

It was my Dad's side of the family that we all gravitated towards, especially our Dublin cousins. I still remember my first trip to Dublin around 1968 with my parents when I was only four years old. We stayed in Inchicore, about four miles west of the city centre, where my Aunt Cha and Uncle Charlie lived, along with their four adult children. My aunt May had a life tenancy there that had been arranged for herself and my grandmother by Pop, before his death in November 1949. My grandmother, Margaret Lucy, had passed away in October 1962, at the age of 85.

Even on that first trip I remember my cousin Raymond, who had such a great sense of humour. The youngest boy, Niall, was always listening to music and singing along to the lyrics. Then there was the eldest boy, Fintan, a soft-spoken man who called me "Lucy Lockett" and always had time to talk to me.

In the summer of 1970, I went with Theresa on another trip to Dublin to stay with our aunts and cousins. The previous year my uncle Charlie had died suddenly, leaving a will that caused much heartache and disunity within the family, for decades to come. It was only later that I learned that Charlie had been very miserly with money and that his family had suffered a great deal because of his obsession. My aunt Cha seemed a lovely woman and this was borne out by everyone. I have memories of her making apple tarts with the apples I'd picked from the orchard at the back of the garden. She was always pleasant but quite reserved. I didn't realise at the time but she had recently been diagnosed with breast cancer and she must have been very worried about the impending surgery.

Raymond was great company. He was into so many fascinating things, like music and books, art and sport. His lifelong passion was for history and, as I got older, he'd bring me around Dublin on summer evenings, walking along the canals or into the city, where my curious eyes were opened to the treasures of the National Art Gallery and the wonders of the National Museum. Then there was Rex, their cuddly Collie that I just adored. The record player must have been on day and night, playing Simon and Garfunkel albums. The melodies were beautiful and I remember humming them all day, trying to make sense of the lyrics.

Sadly, my aunt Cha passed away the following summer, on July 20 1971, at the age of 61. My Dad, my Aunt May and all Cha's family were devastated. It was a very tough time for everyone. My parents attended the funeral in Dublin. Cha's remains were interred in Deansgrange Cemetery, Blackrock. After this sad loss, we saw much more of my aunt May and my cousin Raymond. They stayed with us for Christmas in 1971. I loved playing cards and draughts with Dad and May. Over the years I got to know May's many quirky sides: her jealousy and pessimism that may have had their roots in a failed relationship and in the many disappointments and losses she had endured; her great sense of humour; her undying love for Dublin.

In the summer of 1976, I was allowed to stay with May and Ray in Dublin once again. The atmosphere that I'd remembered as a child had changed after Cha's death. Fintan was married and Niall must have moved out by then. There was tension and angry outbursts there that I wasn't used to in my own home. I figured from the conversations and arguments that there were more problems around Cha's will that were beginning to split the family apart.

Going around the city with May though was always a marvellous experience. She really loved Dublin and her ardour was infectious. Since my first trip to the city as a four-year old, I had also fallen in love with Dublin. It was so exciting to catch a double-decker bus all the way into town, then to browse around the dazzling shops. From day one I loved it all, the beautiful old Georgian buildings, the hustle and bustle of life in O'Connell Street and Grafton Street, the fancy cafes and restaurants, and all the glittering window displays. Eason's was my favourite shop where I'd spend ages searching for books I couldn't get at home. After long periods of browsing, I'd finally select a bundle of books, probably spending most of the money I had in that one store. We'd often have lunch in Woolworths of Henry Street and then we'd stroll across the Halfpenny Bridge, towards Grafton Street and Switzers department store. When we got tired, May brought me into the church in Clarendon Street to light a candle and to have a rest. It was lovely to have had that special time to spend with her in the city.

Often on our way home we'd visit the grotto in the Oblates where we lit candles for all our relatives and said a prayer at my great-granduncle's grave. This was Pop's uncle, Brother William Costigan, who had been a carpenter in the Oblates Church in Inchicore in the nineteenth century. With so many family roots stretching back across the centuries in Dublin, I always felt at home, as though part of me belonged there.

My uncle Joe, Dad's brother, lived with his wife, May, and their son in the old family home in Rosslare Harbour. This was where Dad and his siblings had been reared. Joe followed in his father's footsteps, becoming a train driver and he was also secretary of the Railway Social Club. In Pop's time, the house was owned by The Great Southern and Western Railway and, in 1945, a new State transport company was founded called Córas Iompair Éireann (CIE). The house became the property of CIE and could only be rented by an employee. After Pop's death, Joe was given the option of making his home there, which he did, while my grandmother and May moved to Dublin to live with Cha.

Joe was always very kind and generous. His nieces and nephews loved meeting Joe because he always had silver or notes to dispense. His wife, May, always had sweets stored away in her bag, her favourites being liquorice all-sorts, and she was equally generous sharing these around.

As a child, I only went to visit their home once or twice. I never liked visiting, though their home was very comfortable and well-furnished in every way. For me though, there was a feeling of claustrophobia. It was many years later that I remembered my feelings about the house and finally discovered a valid reason why this might have been. I loved going outside though, running along the cliff with its marvellous views of the sea, climbing down the 99 steps and walking along the beach. It was amazing to sit there and watch, as ships glided in and out of the port. This was the Harbour I savoured but I never wanted to be in the old house.

It was a different era then and children were given much greater freedom. I lived close to the Main Street so, from the age of 8 or 9, I'd saunter down town to look around the shops. Mostly I loved searching for books, especially *The Famous Five* or anything by Enid Blyton; also dolls' dresses and trinkets that I loved to collect. I remember the first time that I saw a row of beautiful decanters, sitting on a shelf in Woolworths. The cut glass sparkled and shone in the light and I set about saving up to buy them. Finally I saved enough and bought the elegant tall one. I set out a small table that I covered with a red velvet cloth, filled the decanter with lemonade and placed it in the centre of the table. I immediately started to save again until the square decanter sat alongside it, filled with a large bottle of coca cola. Next I acquired six glasses from my Dad who had won the set in the Goose Club, a Christmas raffle that was held in the Railway Social Club in Rosslare Harbour every year. Now my set was complete and I could play at being a grand lady, pouring out drinks for my guests.

My fascination with glass didn't stop there, it only continued and grew. When our cousins went on a trip to Italy they arrived back with three rose-coloured decanters from Venice for my parents. They were placed on the Edwardian sideboard that my Dad had inherited from his parents. I loved the way the light caught the coloured glass and reflected its sparkle onto the mirrors behind.

It was also around this time that I began to notice stained-glass windows in churches, the way the sun caught each colour and reflected it like lasers onto walls and floors, creating a magnetising effect. My favourite window was in Clonard Church where Mary was dressed in a deep blue cloak. As a teenager, I often called in there to sit in the stillness and enjoy the beautiful vision, before visiting Theresa and her three boys, Michael, Damien and Paul, who lived close by.

Another event I recall very vividly occurred in 1975 when I was in fifth class in the Faythe School. This sparked my passion for all things from the

1920's. The fifth and sixth classes were taught by the same teacher. The sixth year girls were preparing for a summer concert that would take place in St. Michael's Club. Two of the girls were naturals at singing, acting and comedy. They got together to rehearse a brilliant routine that culminated in a dance that I absolutely loved. I had never heard this type of music before that they played on their tape recorder. That must have surprised me because our home was always full of music. Living through the 1960s and '70s with three grown-up siblings meant that I was open to every kind of sound, from pop, to folk and rock, and everything in between. My parents also loved music. My Dad had played on a band called *The Nighthawks*, touring the dancehalls in the 1940s and '50s. All through my childhood he played music on the piano from those decades. My Mam loved singing songs from the musicals, from the 1930s onwards.

The music I heard that day in school was new to me. The sounds were fast, daring, with deep sassy tones. Neither had I ever seen those sashaying steps but I was dazzled and thrilled, the first time in school I had ever felt excitement and something akin to joy. "It's the Charleston," they announced when the last notes had faded, a dance that had been all the rage fifty years before, in the 1920s.

That morning certainly sowed seeds that I was barely aware of. There was so much from that era that began to fascinate me, those mid-length beaded dresses with fringed skirts, jewelled headbands, long jet black necklaces, cloche hats and boa scarves. I loved the look, the sound and the feeling of fun and freedom that it all evoked. I had no awareness then that the 1920s and all associated with it would later become a major focal point for my understanding of myself, my family and the meaning of life itself.

1. Mike Costigan and Kathleen Rossiter (my parents), Christmas 1950

2. My Dad (Mike Costigan) with baby Anthony on the old strand in Rosslare Harbour, 1954

3. Me, aged 7, 1971

42

4. Pop and Margaret Lucy Costigan (née Flynn) with daughter, Cha McGovern, circa 1938

WEXFORD, FROM 1976

I found my teenage and secondary-school years to be difficult and drab. It was like living in two worlds. At home I was happy, sharing so many hobbies and interests with my mam and dad and my brother, Anthony. We played darts, wrote songs, watched tennis and soccer on TV, and discussed so many subjects. Anthony and I became interested in the paranormal. We tried out ESP (Extra-Sensory Perception) using a pack of cards, each containing a different shape. Anthony would look at the card and try to send a message telepathically to me while I kept my eyes closed, and tried to discern the shape that was on the card. Then we switched places. Some evenings it was amazing when we'd keep coming up with shapes that matched those on the cards.

We all enjoyed watching *Arthur C. Clarke's Mysterious World,* a series that aired on TV in 1980 that brought up many phenomena for us to dissect. We had endless conversations about the Bermuda Triangle, in the western part of the North Atlantic Ocean, where ships supposedly disappeared without trace and about UFOs (Unidentified Flying Objects). I still went to mass, believing in a compassionate, loving Christ, very much in the vogue of *Jesus of Nazareth,* the mini-series that was a smash hit on TV over Easter, 1977.

In school it was a different reality. I was shy and withdrawn. I had few friends and, with those I did have, I was mainly a listener, never sharing anything about my inner world, my opinions, feelings or dreams. I was very fearful of rejection and ridicule, choosing instead to hide and remain largely under the radar. Feeling alienated from your peers may be likened to a slow dripping tap. It may not seem to be doing much damage but over a long period the core becomes eroded, one drop at a time.

In 1980, my Dad retired and sold the business. My aunt May came to live with us for a brief period around then. It didn't work out though because she became dark and moody, finding fault with everyone who tried to make her feel at home. She found an apartment in town and was happier having her own place. Relations became somewhat better then.

There are two highlights I recall from the five years I attended secondary school. The first is going to France on a four-day school tour, stopping off at Rouen Cathedral, in Normandy, and then travelling on to Paris where we visited Notre Dame, the Louvre and the Eiffel Tower. The next great event was discovering F. Scott Fitzgerald's *The Great Gatsby*, written in 1925. Needless to say, I loved the tone and the style of the entire book. It was set in Long Island in the summer of 1922. It deals with the themes of idealism, decadence, social upheaval and excess. I loved reading it, intrigued by the storyline and the characters.

In 1981, the Leaving Certificate results were not available until September, due to an examiner's dispute. I knew once I got those results school would be finished forever. I went up to collect them on a sunny afternoon. When I tore the envelope open I had done just fine and I felt very relieved. More importantly, from that moment on I was free.

As I went about the task of finding my first job and moving into a new phase of life I really had no idea that my family's past held any significance for my current life. There was a vivid recurring dream that I had as a teenager that was sad and poignant but I never discussed this with anyone. I had no psychological tools to analyse anything and certainly no insights to understand what I was feeling or experiencing. Everything seemed pretty ordinary to me, yet, looking back, there were some experiences around that time that would have been worthy of inquiry.

DREAMS AND IMAGININGS

In my teenage years, there was one dream that kept recurring, both as a night dream and a day dream. There was a well-dressed man carrying a bouquet of white roses. It wasn't a happy occasion; that was something I always knew. There was sadness and a lot of it. He was walking towards a grave and it was here that he placed the roses. I'd no idea whose grave it was. I didn't have a clue if this was something real that had taken place or just a sad imagining, maybe a snippet from a book I had read or a film I had seen. There was no colour, just a dark, gloomy atmosphere. It wasn't a disturbing dream, like a nightmare, but, on wakening, the feeling of sadness still lingered. I often thought of it and wondered if it had any significance.

I also thought a lot about Sue, figuring that there were many aspects of life that she had never had the chance to experience. When I thought of Sue, a gloominess would sweep over me. This young girl had had her whole life to live and it was taken from her, becoming a life unfulfilled. I must have been tapping into her pain and sadness as I was reaching my late teens, the same age as when Sue had become ill and went into decline.

Looking back at that time, I was probably in the midst of an existential crisis, trying to figure out the meaning of life, death and suffering. The Catholic tradition I'd been steeped in could do little to answer the question: Why did Sue have to die so young? Following on from this, I didn't find a satisfactory answer to: Why are we here in the first place?

I loved my dad and had great chats with him about many subjects under the sun. Yet, I never felt I could ask him about the sister he had lost all those decades before. I just remember him saying she was a lovely person and everyone was very fond of her. It didn't give me much of a picture of Sue but I had to be content with it.

Going to college in Waterford when I was 19 really widened my horizons and for the first time I felt truly alive. After feeling lonely and inept for much of my teenage years, I finally had a good circle of friends. I had a hectic social life and I was beginning to feel some confidence growing, as I felt liked and respected by my peers. These were the years I began to love dancing and I had some of the best fun ever at the Scholar discos, held in the Bridge Hotel. I hadn't found love just yet but there was no reason to feel I wouldn't meet someone special in time. I believed I was ready to grasp life with both hands and to savour all of its sweetness.

In college, I enjoyed the friendship of classmates and also developed a wider circle. All thoughts of Sue faded, along with the dream of white roses and the man in the throes of sadness. It was a time for living, for truly having fun and sharing camaraderie that was such a great part of college life.

Then, on the cusp of my twenty-first birthday, I began feeling a melancholy again. I felt a nagging anxiety that I didn't understand. It was irrational to feel that I needed to get this birthday out of the way. I remember writing a poem about it. I longed to get to three minutes past twelve on February 9, 1985 when I would be 21. Then I would have achieved something pretty marvellous, certainly a milestone that Sue had sadly never reached.

5. Me, aged 21, 1985

DUBLIN YEARS, FROM 1986

After spending two years studying computing in Waterford and one year in Dundalk, it was time to seek employment. Jobs were hard to come by in the mid-1980s but having computer qualifications made it relatively easy to secure work as a programmer. I had always loved visiting Dublin, so the opportunity to live there was one I relished. In August 1986, I got my chance to work there with a financial institution that was based in the city. It was the start of a whole new chapter. I moved in for a short while with college friends in Leeson Street but finally settled in an apartment in Grosvenor Square, Rathmines, where I remained for 11 years.

I was relieved to have a job and to be earning money again. When I'd first left school I had briefly worked in Wexford as a trainee accountant but, when I began using the computer there, I decided to switch careers and attend college to study computer programming. So, finally settled in Dublin, surrounded by my friends from college, there was only one major problem that began to surface: I didn't actually want to work with computers. It was as though some kind of switch had been turned on and I suddenly realised that I really wanted to work with people, not machines. My childhood dream of being a writer was also simmering away on the back burner so, almost from the day I started work as a programmer, I felt ill at ease. At that time, two-decades before the banking crisis and the major crash that followed, working in a financial institution carried a certain status. The truth for me, however, was that I greatly disliked working in the banking sector and counted the days until I could find a way out. It took until 1997 for me to achieve that goal.

One thing I did love about my work was that it was so centrally located. Also, unlike many other departments, the computer staff were given much greater freedom so I often enjoyed long lunch breaks, meeting friends and family who were visiting, walking down to Grafton Street or even as far as O'Connell Street. I had only been in Dublin a short time when I found the most incredible shop tucked away at the back of the George's Street Arcade, now located at Drury Street. This was Jenny Vander's, a haven for vintage clothing, accessories and jewellery. It was like being transported to another world. Of course, it was the 1920s style that I loved perusing. There were beautiful fringed and beaded dresses in dazzling shades of every colour; long strings of glass beads, classic cigarette holders, a large array of feather boas and wonderful gold and silver fringed bags. Every item was relatively expensive so it was more often a case of browsing than buying.

I also had the opportunity of attending several Christmas parties thrown by the firm that were free to employees. For the first two years I was there, they were held in the magnificent Gresham Hotel on O'Connell Street. This was followed by two parties held in the Royal Dublin Hotel, an establishment that dates back to 1752, located just across the road from the Gresham. The opulence of my first party on a December evening in 1986 was staggering. The best of food and beverages were served in the ornate dining room and this was followed by dancing, well into the early hours of the morning. I had put my hair up and the black dress I wore was certainly reminiscent of the 1920s. The Gresham was so steeped in history, having been the regular lodgings of Michael Collins, after the truce following the War of Independence in the summer of 1921. I guessed I wouldn't have looked too far out of place if I'd suddenly been transported back to that era.

I thought a lot about Sue during my first few years in Dublin. I didn't know much about her, except that she had worked in a golf club in Portmarnock with her sisters. I often wondered, as I browsed in shops, such as Clery's on O'Connell Street, if Sue too had shopped there, trying on hats or jewellery, then going outside and enjoying the rush and buzz of the city.

Despite the surface fun of living in Dublin, in many ways my early twenties were the toughest years of my life. It's sad to think that when there was so much opportunity, when I was so fit and physically well, when I had money and was surrounded by friends in my favourite city, I was not in a good place emotionally. I didn't know where to look or what to do to feel better. I enjoyed the many social aspects of Dublin but, looking back now, there were three major deficits that I was trying to fill: I needed to find some real purpose in my life; I needed to work in an area that was personally fulfilling; and I really wanted to meet someone special and to have a loving relationship.

When I met Philo, I thought I had found true love. He joined the firm where I worked in the summer of 1988 and began working in the computer section. From the first day we met we really hit it off. Tall, dark, intelligent and charming, I loved every moment I spent with him. We had great fun together, taking off the yuppies whose inflated egos were everywhere to be seen where we worked. I lived in Rathmines and had only ever visited friends on the south side but Philo was a North-sider, with family roots deep in the Howth peninsula. Our shared interests included music, history and so many other subjects. Philosophy was his great love, hence his nickname. We speculated so much on the meaning of life that he soon began calling me Sophy, to dovetail with Philo.

We talked and chatted for hours. We walked all over the city, Philo guiding me to the historic areas. Then later, we'd take in a band or a nightclub. I never drank alcohol but I still managed to have the greatest fun ever on those expeditions. *The Legendary Hoods* were probably my favourite of all the bands we went to. They were a brilliant blues and jazz ensemble, playing songs such as *Minnie the Moocher* that dated back to 1931. I couldn't get enough of their deep, rich sound, especially when they played clarinet and saxophone. I loved their style and their flamboyance.

Thinking back to those years, I suppose I was lost in a version of Philo that was so cool, sophisticated and adventurous. I couldn't see the cracks or the problems he was grappling with. I knew there was someone special he couldn't forget, a girl he had loved from the time they were both teenagers. He still met her and, whenever he did, I think the grief of losing her came flooding back.

When Philo was happy he was so great to be with. I remember one lovely summer's day when I visited him in Raheny. We ended up walking into town, past St. Anne's Park, along Clontarf Road where there are marvellous views of the sea, then through Fairview and on into the city. Another day we took the alternate route and walked along Dollymount Strand.

One summer's evening we got the dart to Howth. Philo brought me to St. Mary's Old Abbey Cemetery. He told me his ancestors were buried there and that he'd probably end up there himself. Then he said he was getting thirsty so we'd have to wait for another time to visit St. Fintan's Cemetery, just across the hill in Sutton, where Phil Lynott was buried. It felt so good to head down to the village, to browse around the art shops, to find a quaint restaurant for dinner and to have the whole evening before us.

After that glorious summer's evening in 1989, Philo never did take me to St. Fintan's. It was only recently that I remembered our evening in Howth and how close we'd come to visiting the cemetery. At the time, I hadn't any inkling as to the significance it held for unlocking the final chapter in Sue's and her beau Tom's story.

THE READING

My appointment for a spiritual reading was set for Tuesday, March 27 1990, at 2.30pm. I was informed it would last about an hour and everything would be put on tape. "What exactly is a spiritual reading?" I asked Brendan when I phoned to book an appointment.

"It's channelling your spirit guides. That's what a medium does. It's not reading cards or using any kind of props. Your spirit guides are invited by you to take part."

"Can you see spirits?" I asked, feeling curious but mostly sceptical.

"Yes," he answered without hesitation. "Sometimes the room is filled with so many ancestors who want to step forward to offer love and reassurance. It's a lovely experience."

I turned onto Wicklow Street and found the building I was looking for. I felt apprehensive, still not having a clue what a spiritual reading entailed. I pressed the buzzer and was summoned by Brendan to the top floor. I must have climbed five flights of stairs before I reached the open door that had a plate attached, *Irish Spiritual Movement.*

I had been here for healing a few months previously. Afterwards, I'd definitely felt lighter and life had seemed brighter somehow. My day-to-day reality hadn't changed but I'd begun to see the many options I had and to feel less despondent. So now I was back, to sample my first spiritual reading. Two friends had had readings and they were amazed by the accuracy of what had emerged. So I'd thought it was worth giving it a go.

Brendan met me at the top of the staircase, beaming and making me feel very much at home. His eyes were kind and sparkled with a zest for life. He was a tall, burly man with a grey, shapely beard. He was casually dressed in shirt and jeans with no weird cloaks or other paraphernalia that I might have expected from a spirit medium. I still didn't know what to expect but I felt relaxed and open, yet curious and intrigued by the whole idea that someone could channel spirits and possibly give me insights into aspects of my life.

Brendan led me into his healing room and we both sat down. He poured out a glass of water, then pushed the button on the tape recorder on his desk and began speaking. The following is a transcript of relevant sections of the reading that I was given that day. The only differences are slight changes or omissions due to repetition of words or phrases for ease of comprehension in written form.

"Feel free at any time if you want to interrupt or pull me up, ok? But it will essentially be on the tape."

Brendan began by talking about the importance of the age of seven, a time when children begin on their spiritual path. Then he talked about karma.

"We blame karma on things that happen but karma is actually a very positive thing because it is the goals that we have to achieve, not the punishment that we have to get. But sometimes to achieve those goals we have to go through experiences which can be very uncomfortable and very grim, so consequently we go through quite a rough stage in life. We can make it easy or rough by our understanding of the situation. Sometimes we ignore the signs which have been made abundantly clear to us. Everything is telling us not to buy a particular car, but you go ahead and buy it. It's a wreck, that sort of thing."

"Now the thing too that I want to stress to you is that grim and all that the experiences might have been, they are, would you believe, beneficial to you because they will help you to understand a lot of situations and a lot of people. If you can look back through a lot of experiences in your life to date it will help you have a lot easier future life. In the past, certain events shook you a bit—that's an understatement—but we have to understand that one of the reasons they hit you so badly was that you couldn't communicate them to yourself properly. Somebody poked your favourite teddy's eye out which as a child would be traumatic but now we can sort of laugh at our reaction to it, yet the trauma of an event can still hang on into adult life because we won't face it. We carry the pain of it with us because that teddy is still alive to you."

I hadn't thought about my teddy in years, the one with the eye that had fallen out and had to be sown back in. Brendan's mention of it was uncanny. Also, there had been a number of incidents when I'd been followed home from school by a man who, even at the age of seven, I knew was not a good person.

Once he had grabbed me and tried to kiss me but I ran away. Another day I saw him peering in through my classroom window, pointing over to me in front of teachers and students and I was terrified. I never told anyone. I felt sick with worry in case someone would find out. I thought it was my fault. I wondered if that was what Brendan was referring to. I sat up straight and kept on listening.

"So you have set yourself goals in life. We hear people talk about predetermination and predestination. There's a thing called the inevitability of occurrences and these are the goals you've set in life that you have to achieve. This would be the reason you chose particular paths in life, why you chose to be born in Wexford. Everything that happened to you, you actually chose in some way."

I sat there mystified. Having been raised in the Catholic ethos, I'd never heard any of these concepts before. "When did I choose this?" I asked.

"Before you came down here," he said, looking deeply into my eyes. "Because, you see, you actually chose the moment of your birth. The thing about life is that life is just an intermission and it's rather like in the theatre when you rush out and have a few pints during the intermission, between performances. So too, when you're in the spirit world, you need to make these little excursions into this life to get these experiences to bring back. You've got to understand that life was, is and will be: it is eternal…"

I felt goose bumps crawl up my arms as I sat there. I took a deep breath and waited for more.

"...Not the physical life because you know that you were born and you know you're going to die, so when you know those things you can look on the body and see that it's just a transient vehicle that has only a set span of time. Experiences you've had may be grim from the physical point of view but you look at the spiritual point of view, it's like someone denting or smashing your car and you say, 'Thank God, I'm still alive!' Ok, things will upset you. Last Friday night someone smashed all the windows in my car. My physical reaction is 'I'd love to catch him and teach him a lesson', but my spiritual reaction is, 'I hope he enjoyed it'". Brendan laughs. "Whoever it was needed to get something out of his system."

"You see, the positive side of your experiences is that they can (a) make you an awful lot wiser and (b) make someone else wiser. Then, when you meet someone else who has had a similar experience you can say, 'Ah, don't worry about that, we can sort it out!'"

"So this is what I wanted to say to you, the inevitability of occurrences in everybody's life is not a predestined thing, but it is something that is necessary to happen during the term here on earth and we must be prepared for them because we have set these things ourselves. You see, before we came down here we said, 'I want to experience what it's like to fall out of a tree', 'I want to experience what it's like to be run over by a bus', for whatever spiritual experience you might get from it. But we're here in the physical world and we can enjoy that while we're here. There's nothing which says we must come down and suffer. It's the way that we

60

look on things means that we suffer ourselves. If we could only get on with life, not hold ourselves back or limit ourselves."

Brendan paused to take a sip of water. I was fascinated by what he was saying and just trying to keep up, to take it all in.

"Now, I want to go back with you into past lives."

The mention of past lives completely took me by surprise. I had never thought about this concept before. I was interested though to hear what was coming next.

"There is a relevancy here because it's part of the fact that you escaped experiences in a previous existence that meant you did need to experience them here. This is why they were so intense because they had to be definite experiences. If you could imagine again trying to learn a lesson, you know, 'Don't touch the fire or it'll burn your hand' and you get the poker out of the fire and you don't burn your hand. But you're curious, so the next time you touch the poker further up and it's warm. Eventually, you pick up the red hot tip of the poker and you really cripple yourself. Now, the person responsible for that is you, not the person who put the poker in the fire, not the poker, not the fire. You chose that experience."

"Why we need to experience these things in life is the same reason we were brought into this whole cycle of evolvement. We were part of a spirit revolution, aeons ago. I questioned a lot about this one and I was told to be satisfied with the fall of the angels, that that would be as close as possible to how

61

they could explain it. If you could imagine that we did revolt in the light of perfection, when we realised our own imperceptions. We found we weren't as perfect as we'd thought. But what we felt then was that we weren't entitled to sit by God and be part of the Godhead, so we had to evolve back into that state where we would feel capable of being part of it. So you have already spent two existences trying to assimilate those experiences that you needed and this is why they were so hard for you this time. You have achieved it because here we are talking about it and there's some light being thrown on it for you."

I was hanging on his every word now, enthralled by these concepts.

"Now, the experiences you might relate to are the early part of this century. I don't know if you found that you had an affinity around say the 1920s, because this is in fact where you were in your last incarnation."

I felt a jolt deep inside. My fascination with the 1920s was irrefutable. I hardly dared to wonder what was coming next.

Brendan continued. "You didn't live a very long life, you went off track altogether. It was like an aborted mission and you said, 'Ok, beam me up, Scotty!' You got off early. In fact, you didn't even attain your thirties in that particular life. But in this life you can look to a long life because, from those two past life experiences–the other one was around the start of the last century, you might find that you're interested in the costume of the day or something like that, something historical. You might have a feel for it and then you'll understand that it comes from that part of your existence. Now, it's not normal that one would reincarnate so quickly because we reincarnate in groups. It's not like we all come down the same day but over a period of years we usually come and go, and we usually wait for one another and regroup after every reincarnation."

"In your particular situation there are people of your group who are still living from that time that you were here with last. Now, they would be old because that was about seventy years ago but you could find yourself being in some way related to people living around you still; a grandmother that you would have perhaps been a sister to in a previous existence."

A wave of emotion passed through me when he mentioned the life I had lived where I hadn't reached my thirties. And now he was asking about a living female relative from that life. Immediately I knew who he meant. She wasn't a grandmother but an aunt, a sister who was still living–May, the sister of Susanah's.

"Well, I do have a very old aunt", I said, "and she had a sister who died young and I've always felt something for this person..."

Brendan chuckled. "Well, that's one to check up on. The aunt is still living so you see the link is still there. It was during the hectic twenties anyway, the time of the Charleston and all this sort of stuff, the flappers, so you can find out about that one. Because if it ties in, and I think you will find that it does tie in, it'll help you to understand more about yourself. Ok?"

I sat there speechless and just nodded.

"The other thing that comes up from that time, from long, long ago is a collie dog who is not quite a Lassie type of dog, he's a bit more sophisticated than that, there's a lot of grey, black and white in his coat, and he's long-haired and he has the sharp nose of the collie. I'd say he's the kind of dog you'd want and you did then also have one. I'd put it in the same vagueness, a very misty sort of picture, where things are far away. It's hard to put them together to show you, do you understand? The closer they are the clearer they are and this gives me some idea of why they actually occurred. But this is the past life and again I need to stress to you that this was the way things were."

At this stage I began to feel shocked. I hadn't expected anything when I'd walked in here this afternoon and now it was as though all the questions I'd ever had about purpose and meaning in life were being dished up to me on a platter. It was just too much to take in. Then there was the revelation of a past life: a female relative who had lived a short life in the 1920s. Was I the sister that my Dad and all his family had loved and lost?

Brendan was speaking again.

"There are a few other people here who want to come up. I have somebody who was very involved in sailing. I have a funny feeling that this person was not from your present life but from a previous time. This person came in on the same vibration as your aunt. It's not sailing in regatta; it's sailing as in seafaring. He's brightly dressed in the classic dress of the sailing-ship time which would have been around the turn of the century. You might find that there is some relative from that time that again your old aunt might throw some light on."

I interjected here. "My great-grandfather was supposed to have spent quite a long time at sea".

Brendan nodded. "Yeah, it could be that alright. He has his little straw hat, with the little ribbon on it and the two little tassels hanging down the back. The jacket is a short jacket and the trousers are cream-coloured, the colour of a candle. I'm conscious of a lot of people there because there seems to have been a history of large families in your ancestry and consequently there's a strong link with those families."

Brendan took another sip of water, then continued. "Now, in this life you were sort of squashed in. There was a facility made for you to come back. Maybe your mother mightn't have told you. I don't know how open she is about it", he laughed. "When you got to the other side and you realised, 'Oh! I shouldn't be here yet', there was a gap made for you to squeeze back in here. You'll find this perhaps in relation to the rest of the family. Maybe you weren't expected or maybe you surprised everybody. But it was to facilitate you to come back and to have another go and you've made a good job of it–hard and all as it has been–but you can be pleased about that."

I sat there stunned. I was aware of Mam's three losses during pregnancies before I was born and the way I surprised everyone, even my siblings when I was born.

"So, just to bring you roughly back over it. Check on the aunt. It was past experiences

65

unfulfilled that brought you into this life, that led you into the difficulties of this life and that have now gone behind you, but they will need to be properly boxed, understood and categorised."

"Ok!" Brendan smiled. "This leaves very little to tidy up. Again, a long life, a very long life and a great deal of happiness…"

Outside, the city was bustling but I hardly saw or heard anything. I wondered how I would go back to work and sit through the mediocrity of finishing the programme I had been working on before lunch. I would have to tell someone what I'd experienced. The scepticism I had felt on entering the building that day had been utterly eradicated. I felt light yet overwhelmed; giddy with excitement and full of questions. If I thought I had problems before the reading, how was I now going to cope with this startling revelation? One thing was for sure, I needed to find out everything I could about my aunt, Susanah Costigan.

IF YOU KNEW SUSIE

I listened again to the reading over the next few days. It was uncanny how accurate I felt Brendan had been about so many things, not only about the enormous revelation about a possible past life–that most certainly referred to my Aunt Sue in the 1920s– but also about many other aspects of my life. Brendan also offered me great insights and guidance.

He spoke about my deepest core: having a beauty and sensitivity that so far I couldn't share with anyone for fear of being hurt; the reasons why relationships had been so difficult; about the person I would eventually meet in the future who would share my sensitivity and allow me to show my true self, a person with whom I could share beautiful moments, without fear of rejection. He also described a future scene where he saw me opening a window and letting in the sunlight, signifying a new stage of life where I would be happy and fulfilled, living an authentic life, where the difficulties of the past would be just distant memories. I was still dazed by the enormity of it all. In just one hour, my mind had been opened to spiritual teachings and concepts that I had never before even heard of.

The big bombshell of course had been the assertion that I was the reincarnation of my aunt, Sue. This played on my mind a lot and I found it difficult to come to terms with. I didn't know anyone in my circle that might have a clue about such esoteric matters. I planned to do some of the workshops on spirituality advertised in the Spiritual Centre and to look up books that might give me another perspective on what I was dealing with here. I needed to find answers that would satisfy me, one way or the other, around the whole area of reincarnation and, more specifically, whether or not I had actually lived a previous life as my Dad's sister.

When I went home to Wexford the weekend after the reading I was trying to play it cool. I was bursting to tell everyone what I'd found out but I knew that wasn't the sensible thing to do. It was only many years later that I mentioned to my parents, to Theresa and Anthony, and to Raymond that I had visited a spirit medium who had told me I had lived a previous life as Sue. For the moment though, I had to keep all that under wraps. It was simply too enormous to divulge to anyone who hadn't gone for a reading themselves and had experienced first-hand the accuracy of what Brendan had divulged.

Although I had a very close relationship with my Dad, the Ireland of 1990 hadn't awakened enough to openly discuss alternative views on spirituality or even the possibility of past lives. We were still well and truly in the throes of Catholicism. I couldn't blame anyone for being sceptical because I hadn't ever considered past lives, until the startling revelations began to unfold in the reading, the previous week. I figured, it would be much simpler to casually inquire about my ancestors and then to focus in on Sue. In many ways I felt like a detective, beginning to gather evidence to see if it correlated with Brendan's reading or if it refuted his interpretation of events in anyway.

Beginning with Brendan's reference to a seafaring ancestor who came from the same time as Sue, there was little doubt that this was my great-grandfather–and Sue's grandfather–Michael Flynn, the shipwright who had sailed on the high seas. May remembered he had lived in East Square, Inchicore, Dublin, with his daughters, Charlotte and Eileen, and the Deegan family. Recently, now that records have been digitised, I found that Michael Flynn had been living in East Square until his death in 1920 at the age of 67, when Sue was aged 11. He was indeed from the same era as Sue, though the main part of his life had been lived in the nineteenth century.

Of course, I was most eager to bring the conversation around to Sue. I had never seen a photo of her so it was uppermost on my mind to find one. My Dad didn't possess one, nor did May. After all that had been revealed, I was bitterly disappointed not to be able to see what she had looked like. It would take me another few weeks before I tracked down three photos of Sue that my cousin Raymond discovered, in his home in Inchicore. They had been kept safely tucked away for all the years by Sue's sister, Cha, who was now sadly deceased.

The following is the account I got from my Dad, my aunt May and from Cha's son, Raymond, on that weekend and also during further conversations and correspondence over the intervening years. Sue was the middle child of Margaret Lucy Flynn from Cork and Michael Nicholas Costigan, known as Pop, from

Dublin. Sue was born on October 4 1911 in Ballygeary, Rosslare Harbour and was registered as Sussanna Frances Costigan. The first name on her birth certificate was probably a misspelling as she always spelt her name Susanah. Her older sisters were May, aged four and Cha, aged two. Her mother had always yearned for a son and she got her wish when Michael, my dad, was born three years after Sue, on February 2 1914. A second son, Joseph, followed on April 16 1916, just a week before the Easter Rising in Dublin.

As an aside, Joe was born at the home of the Deegan's in 16 East Square, Inchicore. The Easter Rising began the following week on April 24. During the week-long rebellion, martial law was enforced and it became incredibly dangerous to travel anywhere, as British troops combed the city, in search of republican fugitives. When Pop arrived in Dublin, he had a lot of trouble getting through the British army checkpoints. At Mount Brown, in Kilmainham, he was stopped and questioned, as his identity seemed to be suspect. Luckily, a policeman vouched for him and confirmed that he was Train Driver Costigan who had originally lived in Bow Lane. Otherwise, he could have been arrested or executed on the spot, like so many other innocent civilians.

Fortunately, life was much quieter for the family in Rosslare Harbour. The girls were educated at the Mercy Convent and later at the Presentation Convent in Wexford. It was May's responsibility to look after the younger children, particularly the boys. The beach provided endless entertainment for the children and they always had a dog in the house, first Dan and then Dash, to bring for walks along the strand. The great pastime was to sit on the bank, watching the steam ships as they glided in and out of the harbour. Mike loved swimming and, as he grew older, he often dived off the Pier, far into the sea below. Sue was particularly athletic and loved running. In the evenings the family enjoyed playing cards and draughts.

Their mother, my grandmother, was very devout and made sure that the family attended all religious ceremonies. She was kept busy running her home and looking after the long-term lodgers she took in. She was quite witty but also cutting and loved nothing better than to sit at her bedroom window, doling out nick-names for her unsuspecting neighbours. The boys always got the best of everything. Dad was particularly bright at school and was very talented musically so, by all accounts, he was her favourite. May, the eldest daughter, had a special connection with her mother and also enjoyed a favoured status.

Pop had a great sense of humour. He had a horse and trap and used it to bring his family and his elderly neighbours to mass on Sundays. He loved to joke and he enjoyed nothing better than a sing-song. He appears to have had a very soft spot for his youngest girl, Sue. He loved singing this song to her:

I come from Alabama
With a banjo on my knee
I'm going to Louisiana,
My true love for to see.

It rained all night the day I left
The weather it was dry
The sun so hot, I froze to death
Susanna, don't you cry.

Oh, Susanna,
Oh don't you cry for me
For I come from Alabama
With a banjo on my knee...

May left school at the age of fourteen and became apprenticed to a seamstress in Wexford, where she remained for a year. Cha was apprenticed to Fallon's confectioners in Clonmel. Pop paid a half crown a week for Cha's training and she became an excellent baker and confectioner. After being there a year, Cha became homesick and returned to the Harbour. In the early 1920s, in such a troubled political landscape, unemployment was rife and so it was difficult to place the two eldest girls.

Pop had always remained on good terms with his Dublin relations. His eldest sister, Mary Anne, had married Joe McDonagh and lived in a large house at 54 Old Kilmainham, Inchicore. Mary Anne gave birth to twelve children, although only eight survived past infancy. In 1912, her eldest daughter, Kathleen, married a British army officer, Jim Carr from Belfast. The Carrs spent several years in Risalpur in India before returning to Dublin in 1921. They immediately applied for positions as Steward and Stewardess of the Pormarnock Golf Club, were successful in their endeavours and took up their duties in 1922.

Kathleen and Jim remained childless and recently, Kathleen had suffered another miscarriage. Her sister, Margaret Waters, known as Missie, gave birth to her fifth child on February 18 1922, at 17 Turvey Avenue. An arrangement was struck between the sisters, whereby the Carrs, fearing they would never have their own child, adopted the ten-day old boy, naming him Joseph Benedict. This was most fortuitous for Joe as he began playing golf as a young boy in the club. This early training, combined with his innate ability, set him on course for a remarkable career as an amateur golfer.

In Joe Carr's autobiography, *Breaking 80*, he described the shame he felt at not being the natural son of the Carrs, who were his parents, as far as he was concerned. This was the era when so much was swept under the carpet and Joe's parentage was treated in a similar manner, as the Carrs never addressed the issue. In later life, the situation was so upsetting for Joe that he changed his name from Waters to Carr by deed poll.

In 1922, at the height of the Civil War, the Carrs moved into their new quarters at Portmarnock Golf Club and immediately set about hiring staff. Soon after their appointment, Kathleen and Jim drove to Rosslare Harbour to visit their uncle. Their arrival caused great commotion when they drove into the village, in the car they had been given as part of their contract at Portmarnock. When discussing the Costigan girls' future, Kathleen informed Pop that they required a waitress/barmaid for the club and that they were prepared to offer the position to May.

The package included accommodation, food and a nominal wage.

The distance that May would have to travel was one-hundred and thirteen miles in total. The railway line had been installed in Rosslare Harbour from 1911, running along the east coast, arriving in Amiens Street Station, now Connolly Station, in Dublin. On arrival, May would then get a train to Portmarnock station. She would then be collected by the Carrs or another staff member and be driven to Portmarnock.

The Civil War between the Free State and the Anti-treaty forces had begun in June 1922. This must have been a real worry for Pop, particularly as he had been caught up in the aftermath of the 1916 rising in Dublin and knew how quickly an innocent bystander could be embroiled in a life-threatening situation. The Carrs, however, promised to take very good care of May.

Although May was only 15, she jumped at the chance. She was delighted to work for her cousins in the illustrious golf club, taking on bar duties, domestic chores and also looking after the infant, Joe. Perhaps she savoured the freedom and status that a paid position would give her, instead of working as a babysitter, cleaner and cook at home.

As an aside, Pop's old neighbour from James Street, W. T. Cosgrave became President of the Executive Council from 1922 to 1932. In May 1923, the Civil War ended with a victory for the Free State. Peace, law and order began to prevail. In 1924, when Cha reached the age of 15, she was also invited by Kathleen Carr to join May in Portmarnock. Cha readily accepted. The young Joe Carr took a great shine to Cha and a strong bond developed between them. Both May and Cha got on really well in the golf club. Every few weeks they travelled back to the Harbour, regaling their younger sister, Sue, with stories of the many illustrious clients who frequented the club and filling her full of longing to share in the adventures they had in the city.

Sue was still at home, looking after her brothers and whiling away her time, desperately missing her sisters. She yearned to get the chance to join them in Portmarnock. By all accounts, Sue was a very good-humoured, fun-loving and popular girl. Her parents didn't want to inquire if there was work for her in Dublin as they felt the house would be deserted without her. Sue had to bide her time, spending her evenings reading or listening to radio broadcasts that began in Ireland in 1925. The family loved nothing better than to listen to news programs and concerts. The world was rapidly changing with new inventions, modern fashions with short, drop-waisted dresses, and new exciting sounds such as jazz and ragtime. There was one special song from 1925 that Sue loved to dance to:

> *If you knew Susie, like I know Susie*
> *Oh! Oh! Oh! What a girl...*

The singer facetiously sings that Susie is much wilder and more daring than anyone might imagine. Perhaps this reflected Sue's desire to seek out adventure with her sisters in Dublin.

Finally, in 1927, at the age of 15, Sue got her chance to work in Portmarnock. She was bursting with excitement as she accompanied her sisters on the train journey that would take her to a whole new life. Sue's Dublin chapter was about to burst open.

Research Facility - Birth Record

Chláir Uimhir Registration Number: **10060781**

i gComhar an Chláraitheora Maoirseachta in the Superintendent Registrar's District of: **Wexford**

Breith a Chláraíodh i gCeantar Birth Registered in the district of: **Broadway**

i gComhar in the County of: **Co. Wexford**

Uimh.	Dáta of Birth Date of Birth	Ainm Name	Gnéas Sex	Ainm, Sloinne agus Ionad Chónaithe an Athar Name and Surname and Dwelling-Place of Father	Ainm agus Sloinne an Máthar agus a sloinne roimh phósadh dí Name and Surname and Maiden name of Mother	Céim nó Gairm Bheatha an Athar Rank or Profession of Father	Síniú, Cáilíocht agus Ionad Chónaithe an Fhaisnéiseora Signature, Qualification and Residence of Informant	An Dáta a Chláraíodh When Registered	Síniú an Chláraitheora Signature of Registrar	Ainm Baiste nái tugadh e tar-éis chláru na Breithe agus an Dáta Baptismal Name: if added after Registration of Birth and Date
349	19 fourth October 1911 Ballygeary	Susanna F Frances	F	Michael Costigan Ballygeary	Lucy Costigan Nymon	Eugene Bride	Lucy Costigan Mother Ballygeary	Twenty fourth November 1911	Gerrard James H Quigln Registrar	

6. Sue Costigan's Birth Certificate

Portmarnock Golf Club, Portmarnock.

7. Portmarnock Club House, circa 1911

8. Portmarnock Golf Club Dining Room, circa 1911

9. Sue, Tom and Cha at Portmarnock Golf Club, circa 1929

10. Jane Morris née Burden (1839-1914)

PORTMARNOCK GOLF CLUB, FROM 1927

The weekend after the reading, I heard for the first time the scant details that could still be recalled of Sue's years in Dublin. Over sixty years had passed since the three sisters had worked together in the Portmarnock Golf Club. When I asked my aunt May about that time, she said it was the happiest of her life. Although Sue spent just four years in Portmarnock, this was where she truly blossomed. There was the camaraderie and banter to enjoy with her co-workers; the many ups and down experienced while attending to the club's most elite clients; then dancing to the sound of jazz bands in Dublin City, well into the early hours of the morning. It was also where Sue fell in love, for the first and only time in her short life.

I finally got my first glimpse of Sue, pictured beside her boyfriend, Tom, and her sister, Cha. It was probably taken by May. It was a borrowed moment between three colleagues on a smoking break in the car park, located beside the golf club. Perhaps they are sharing some snippet of gossip from the night before or just catching up on one another's day. So many photos from bygone years depict subjects in formal clothing, looking stiff and self-conscious. For most people, photography was a new phenomenon, something to be curious about but also slightly fearful. This couldn't be more in contrast with the photo of this threesome.

Positioned on the left, Sue radiates self-assurance, staring straight into the camera lens, posing with left-hand poised on her hip while she takes a puff of her cigarette. She looks as though nothing could possibly faze her, yet she couldn't have been more than 18. She is every bit the epitome of the flapper, with her short bobbed hair and pretty dark features.

On the right-hand side, Cha smiles as she leans in towards Tom. Her cigarette is held in her left-hand. I had only known Cha when she was in her late 50s and I never guessed that she had possessed such a striking beauty in her youth. The likeness to Jane Burden Morris, muse to Rossetti and poster-girl of the Pre-Raphaelites, is unmistakable. Both Sue and Cha are dressed in black dresses and tights, though Sue's dress appears to be shorter than Cha's.

Tom, in the middle, has his arms loosely draped across both girls' shoulders. The camera has caught Tom with his eyes closed as he breathes out the smoke he has just inhaled. These are three friends who know each other well and are comfortable in each other's company. It reminds me of how tiny moments shared can be so precious.

From recently doing some research, I found that the Portmarnock Golf Club dates back to 1894, developed on the peninsula that is just two miles long, on 500 acres. The peninsula is made up of low sand dunes, grass hollows and long valleys. The club had a reputation for employing workers who lived close by. It was always a rule that membership was only open to men and that ladies could not even attain associate membership. Female visitors did golf there and ladies championships were held since the early 1900s. However, the all-male membership rule still prevails in the twenty-first century, maintaining the club's elitist status.

The first club house burned down in 1905 and was rebuilt in 1906. Gas was installed in 1914 and a wind-driven electric generator was positioned on the small hill beside the car park, providing electric power. The new building had a member's lounge, a bar and a dining room, two changing rooms, a kitchen and a workshop for professionals. There were further extensions completed in 1927, including the addition of a card room. Upstairs, there were bedrooms allocated for six staff members, along with the Carr's private quarters. This was the clubhouse that Sue worked in.

In August, 1927, the first official open championship in Ireland was hosted by the club. This is probably why Sue was employed that summer, just in time for the competition, as many golfing enthusiasts from all over the country were expected to attend. The prize fund was £1,000. The weather turned nasty for the final round, with a gale blowing and rain bucketing down. Kathleen Carr came up with the idea of collecting as much brown paper as she could and giving it to George Duncan to line his clothes, to keep out the cold and the rain.

Duncan managed to defeat his competitors as well as the elements to win the competition.

It was always a club frequented by men of wealth and privilege: colonels, successful business owners, members of the clergy and those who ranked among the country's most illustrious graduates in law, medicine and dentistry. The finest of food and wines were served at lunch and dinner. No doubt, there was fine silver and cut-glass crystal used for special occasions. May always spoke with great fondness of the club, referring to the distinguished clients she served there as 'our betters'. This was the lasting effect on May of that upper class entitlement that permeated every facet of life in Portmarnock.

Sue was appointed as waitress and helped out with other duties, such as working in the bar when requested. She also minded Joe Carr, who was aged five when she began working there. Raymond filled me in on a phone conversation he had with Joe Carr, when Joe was in his 80s. Joe still recalled the three Costigan girls who had had a hand in his rearing when he was a child in Portmarnock.

On their days off, the girls often travelled across the city to visit their cousins, the Deegans, in East Square, Inchicore. There was also the glamour of window shopping in Clery's and Arnott's. This was the time of the flappers, when Dublin's social life was hectic and varied, with numerous dance halls, theatres and cinemas. Dublin had many attractions to amuse three young, fun-loving girls. It was the great age of cinema with such stars of the silent screen as Charlie Chaplin, Mary Pickford, Douglas Fairbanks, Gloria Swanson, Harold Lloyd,

Clara Bow and Rudolph Valentino. *The Jazz Singer* (1927), the first talkie film made by Warner Brothers, was a much anticipated event when first screened. The girls loved La Scala Theatre and Opera House, where opera, cinema and theatre were performed. This was located behind the Metropole, beside the GPO on O'Connell Street.

The girls loved to travel on the electric trams, right into the heart of the city. They often brought their aunt's dog, Jack, with them on their excursions. They all loved Jack, their big cuddly chaperone. Cha reminisced to Ray of learning to dance the Charleston with Sue in city dance halls and of their delight in mastering the steps. *The Charleston* first appeared in the Broadway musical, *Runnin' Wild* in 1923 and became the hit of the decade. My dad recalled that Sue had always been athletic and a very fast runner. In Dublin, she channelled all that athleticism into dancing. May loved to talk of afternoons when the three of them would get dressed up and go out for tea, then pay a penny to dance with professional dancers who would show them the latest steps.

In the area of romance, Sue, the youngest, was the first to find a beau. He was none other than Tom, the maintenance man in the golf club. Sue and Tom quickly fell in love and spent every second they could together. Tom also had a market garden that he cultivated at his home in Sutton. Dad remembered him as a very pleasant and charming man. He was of medium height, had dark wavy hair and shared Sue's love of dancing and athletics. He had a motorbike and took part in races along the strand at

Portmarnock. The couple seemed to have a very happy future in store.

The girls still travelled home to Rosslare Harbour whenever they had holidays. In 1928, their mother took in a boarder named Andrew. During that time May became very attached to him. Andrew was part of the clerical staff in CIE and he was very active socially in the Harbour, being involved in theatricals and sport. He played a leading role in the popular opera *The Bohemian Girl*, in which May and my Dad also took part. Whenever May was home, Andrew invited her on trips around the county and they enjoyed playing tennis together. After a period of time they became engaged. The engagement, however, was short lived. According to my dad, Andrew's parents in Celbridge, Co. Kildare, were quite snobbish and they had always looked to their son to support them financially. They didn't approve of the marriage and persuaded Andrew to withdraw from the engagement. He did so and immediately applied for a transfer from Rosslare Harbour.

This event affected May very badly. Even decades later, she refused to talk to her family about her heartache. Raymond, who had lived with his aunt all his life, never heard May mention her short engagement. He did, however, recall the ring that May donated to the Oblate's when there was a request for gold jewellery. The gold was melted down and used to make the crown of Our Lady that is positioned above the entrance to the grotto in Inchicore, a replica of the grotto in Lourdes. Raymond, in hindsight, believed that this must have been the fate of May's engagement ring.

While May nursed a broken heart, Sue's romance blossomed. Tom travelled with Sue to the Harbour to meet her family and he was a big hit with them all. In March 1931, the Costigans took in another boarder, Charles Francis McGovern. On visits back home, Cha caught the eye of Charlie and they began going out together.

Shortly after Charlie's arrival in the Harbour, Sue was forced to return home. She had got a bad cold in Portmarnock and her doctor advised that her tonsils be removed. The operation was performed in Wexford. Tom visited her there. Before her throat had fully healed, Sue insisted on riding to Rosslare Harbour on the back of Tom's bike. Her health rapidly deteriorated.

Tuberculosis (TB) was a highly infectious disease that was spread through the inhalation of certain bacteria. It was rampant in Ireland at this time. According to the Irish Red Cross Journal, 12,000 young adults died of TB in Ireland in 1904. At its peak, it ravaged families and communities. There was scant knowledge of how to stop its spread and every age-group was effected. Sue had sadly caught this lethal disease and she rapidly went into decline.

It was out of the question that she could return to work. It was heart-breaking for the family to see Sue fading away. On sunny afternoons, she was allowed to sit in the garden reading, wrapped up in a heavy coat and hat.

Every time I look at the photo of Sue in the garden I feel sad. She looks so solitary, all wrapped up in her heavy coat with the fur collar and cuffs. Her face is mainly obscured by her hat as she continues to read. After having just three fun-years in Dublin, this is what her life had shrunk to, a short respite in the sun. I wondered then what was the book she was reading. That question would be answered in time.

Cha left Portmarnock to nurse Sue but nothing could be done to restore her health. May continued to work in Portmarnock but she spent every weekend she could with her sisters. Tom and Sue wrote to each other every week, though none of their letters have survived.

Everything was tried to find a cure for Sue. Many doctors' opinions were sought but nothing could be done. Strange brews and treatments were tried, such as persuading their wilting daughter to drink animal's blood in a final attempt to save the ashen, weakening girl, who was coughing up blood and fading fast in front of their eyes. Even the wealthiest family in the parish, the Murphy's of Kilrane, couldn't save their daughter from the ravaging effects of TB, even when they sent her for treatment to a sanatorium in Switzerland.

Sue died on 18th March 1932 at the age of twenty. Immediately afterwards, Pop went out for a walk alone, to try to deal with his grief. It was the second tragic death of a daughter that he had to endure, having been also present when Baby Catherine succumbed to convulsions at only five months old.

The Costigan household found it very difficult to cope. Both parents became ill with grief. My Dad rarely spoke about this time. Once only he did confide, that both he and Joe had felt helpless, as they couldn't make up in any way for Sue's loss. The girls grieved deeply as they had been so close to Sue in every aspect of her life. The whole village was in shock. A notice of sympathy was posted in *The People* from the Rosslare Harbour Co-Operative Society. The Gaelic League postponed its weekly language classes as a mark of respect.

Tom was really devastated when he heard the news. After turning 25 the previous week, life should have been bursting with happy plans and fine prospects. Instead, Tom travelled the long journey to Sue's funeral in Kilrane, placing on her grave a bouquet of white roses.

11. Sue in the garden of Rosslare Harbour, 1932

12. The Costigan children, c. 1920

MAKING SENSE OF IT ALL

I returned to work the following Monday, still trying to make sense of all I had learned of Sue's short life and her early death. The enormity of the situation began to hit home. Had I really lived that life as Sue or was there another explanation for my feeling of connection to my aunt and the 1920s? Her tragic death really affected me. She had found love and had seemed so happy and yet it had all dissolved around her. And what of Tom, I wondered? What became of him? Did he pine away after losing Sue or did he pick up the pieces and find another love?

The facts that Brendan had outlined in the reading had been largely verified by my family. Sue had lived in the height of the 1920s. She hadn't attained her 30s, in fact dying at the age of 20. Her siblings were still alive from that time, all except her sister, Cha. In this life, my mother had a stillbirth and two miscarriages before I was born, dovetailing with Brendan's description of a gap having been made for me to squeeze back in here, as though my birth was unexpected and a surprise to many.

I pondered whether Brendan had channelled all these facts from the spirit world or whether he was tapping in to some greater consciousness, such as an ancestral memory. I wondered if there might be some psychological or scientific theory to explain memories or impressions from one lifetime being filtered down to a relative in another life. As this was 1990, the world of the Internet was only in its infancy and was not yet available in Ireland. So I began to search in bookstores where I turned up nothing of significance.

I did find something of interest though in my local library: The concept of the collective unconscious that was originally proffered by psychoanalyst, Carl Jung. In *Archetypes and the Collective Unconscious*, Jung put forward the theory that part of the unconscious mind is genetically inherited and is responsible for our deep seated beliefs and instincts, such as sexuality and spirituality. It was a long way though from an explanation of how actual memories or experiences could be passed down through decades from an aunt to a niece. Whatever had happened during my reading with Brendan, it was way out of my experience and, as of yet, I wasn't sure what to make of it.

I was certain that I had mentioned nothing whatsoever to Brendan, either before or during the reading, that could have linked me to Sue or to the 1920s. No one among my circle of friends knew anything about my aunt who had died young. I had never discussed my family history with anyone as it had never come up in conversation.

Also, there was no way of just calling this a lucky guess or a coincidence. All the times that I had been moved by the style, music and dances of the 1920s were undeniable. I wondered about my childhood fascination with glass decanters–had this been a flashback to Sue's years in Portmarnock, serving drinks for those wealthy clients? Then there were my feelings of apprehension when I was approaching the age of 21, as though I feared I wouldn't make it. Was this to do with Sue's death at the age of 20, that was actually my death in a previous life?

It sickened me to think that Sue had to drink animal's blood in a final effort to survive. Had that anything to do with my revulsion of meat and my vegetarian diet since childhood? I remember very well when I stopped eating meat as a young child, when I realised it had something to do with blood. I think I may have had a phobia around blood, as I also fainted on several occasions as a child when I saw blood, once when I was visiting a relative in hospital. I had always known I wasn't material for a career in nursing or medicine.

I also thought of the easy, loving connection, I'd always had with my dad. It was one of peers hanging out together, like brother and sister, rather than a heavy father-daughter relationship. Again, it all fit together so well. Brendan had also mentioned a type of dog, a Collie, that Sue loved and that I would be drawn to. I loved dogs, particularly collies. I wondered if the special dog in Sue's life had been Jack, the big cuddly chaperone that had accompanied the three Costigan girls on many of their outings to the city.

Of course, the most spine-tinging revelation of all was the mention of white roses. Both May and Dad recalled this sad fact. So it was Tom who had put the bouquet of white roses on Sue's grave. The dream that had resurfaced from time to time and had puzzled me for so long had real meaning–Tom's final act of love for his sweetheart.

Then there was the incident in college when a friend had arrived in Dundalk on his motorbike. Everyone had gathered around and eyed his machine with envy. Ben asked if I'd get on and go for a spin around town with him. I was embarrassed to turn him down but I just couldn't do it. There was something that kept telling me to steer clear of motor bikes. Was this a memory from my past life when the last time Sue was on Tom's motorbike she caught cold, a costly error of judgement that had led to her early demise? I knew that Sue had loved going on excursions with Tom on his bike. She had been adventurous and daring, qualities I certainly didn't possess in this lifetime.

I felt so many conflicting feelings then: definitely sadness for a life unfulfilled; confusion whether that life could be claimed as mine or whether some other explanation could be presented; excitement that if this was all true, then death was just a transition to another world and life really was eternal.

I also pondered the second past life that Brendan had referred to, around the beginning of the last century, the 1800s. My fascination with the Pre-Raphaelites as a form of art fitted more with the mid-1800s, as I was certainly drawn to the clothing and style of that time. The writers I most enjoyed were the Brontës, Charlotte (1816–1855) and Emily (1818–1848), based in Yorkshire, in the romantic era of art and literature in the early 1800s. It was just something else for me to consider.

I met my cousin, Raymond, quite frequently in the following weeks. I told him I was interested in finding out more about my aunt, Sue. I hadn't confided anything about the reading yet to my family so my probing for information was in the context of genealogy. Raymond was most helpful, not only telling me stories and anecdotes that his mother Cha had passed onto him but also bringing me tangible items that Sue had owned, such as her draughts set and board, inscribed with her distinctive signature. Ray also gave me a photo of the Costigan children from around 1920, taken in the Plantation in Rosslare Harbour.

This was certainly a subdued photo. May, the eldest at around 12 years of age, is positioned at the back of the group. Cha, aged 10, stands to her left, while Sue, probably 8 years old, is at the right-hand side. My dad, Mike, aged around 6, is seated in front. Joe, aged 4, is standing beside him. None of the children are smiling. Sue is wearing a plain dress, stockings and sensible shoes. Her dark hair hangs down to her shoulders, kept in place with a hairband. She wears a simple necklace. All of the family had deep blue eyes but that detail is sadly missing. It is a great photo to have of the five siblings, yet there is no sparkle or fun anywhere to be seen. They were probably warned to stay still and to stand up straight, while the photographer set up the camera and glass plates.

I was also keen to learn more about Cha and to know what had become of the Carrs. One evening, Ray invited me back to his home in Inchicore. I hadn't been there since my teenage years. We talked a lot about his mother. After Sue's death, Cha had found some solace in Charlie McGovern's growing affection for her. He began taking her out to dances, for trips around the county and bought her expensive gifts. Ray produced his father's pocket diary that dated from that time. In it, Charlie had listed some of the gifts he had purchased for Cha, along with the cost of each item: a pair of black gloves (one pound and six shillings), a gold wristlet watch (four pounds and ten shillings), a manicure set (eighteen shillings and six pence), a platinum powder box (seven shillings and six pence) and fair-face cream (two shillings). He also bought gifts for the other members of the family and was very much liked by them all. I suppose there was no way of knowing at the time that this was an investment for Charlie and that spending lavishly on anyone would never be repeated.

Charlie and Cha became engaged on August 19 1934. For this occasion, he presented Cha with an 18 Carat platinum-set diamond ring that cost twelve pounds. This was still a time when the Catholic Church had an enormous grip on people's lives, especially in small rural villages. Fr. Kinsella, the parish priest, became very unhappy because the engaged couple were living in the same house when they were not married, as, he said, there was obvious temptation. He talked to Mrs. Costigan about the situation. As Margaret Lucy was a stringent churchgoer, she encouraged her daughter to marry as soon as possible, so as not to upset the clergy or the neighbours.

Before the wedding, Charlie got word that he was to be transferred to Sligo. Pop asked Charlie to let Cha remain in Rosslare Harbour until he had set up a home for them in Sligo. On Tuesday, February 4 1936, Charles Francis McGovern and Charlotte Lucy Costigan were married in Kilrane Church, Rosslare Harbour. Charlie bought Cha an 18 carat gold wedding ring for the occasion. A large reception was held in the family home. Charlie later wrote in his diary that it was one of the greatest days of his life. Pop's relations arrived from Dublin, including his niece, Teaso McDonagh. Jim and Kathleen Carr drove from Portmarnock to celebrate the occasion.

The happy couple honeymooned in Torquay, Brighton and in London and had a very enjoyable time. However, the first real row occurred on their honeymoon when Cha asked for an allowance of £1 per week and Charlie refused to give it. The problem of Charlie's meanness with money, that he had kept hidden from everyone during his courtship, continued unabated throughout their marriage, causing great unhappiness. This was accompanied with violent bursts of temper. As a result, Cha had a very hard life, struggling to keep the family fed, clothed and protected.

My Dad told me about Charlie's family, how he had been born in Joliet, Chicago, Illinois, where his father had worked as a floorwalker or supervisor in a department store. When Charlie was six years old, his father, as the eldest son, was summoned back to Glangevlin, in Co. Cavan to take over the family farm, a poor land where it was difficult to eke out a decent living. Charlie's childhood was greatly impoverished, when his father died, leaving a widow and a large family. Dad surmised that this must have had a detrimental effect on him. Charlie was the eldest and struggled to work on the farm while also attending to his studies. The adult Charles McGovern sought to save whatever money he earned, leaving a legacy of enforced poverty and conflicting attitudes about money to his children.

According to his diary, Charlie felt very sad and lonely to be in Sligo without his, "darling, sweetest wife". He rented a flat in Sligo and Cha moved there to be with him. Cha, however, greatly disliked both the town and its inhabitants. In February 1938, they moved back to Dublin and set about buying a home. They finally saw a large house they liked in Inchicore, Dublin 8. Cha and Charlie bought the house and began rearing their family there. Mike and Joe kept a close eye on things and always tried to help Cha out as best they could. They never knew the extent of her misery though as this only fully emerged after her death.

Later, when Pop retired, Charlie approached him to use his retirement lump sum of £300 as a loan to Charlie to enable him to pay off the remainder of the mortgage on the house. In return, Charlie would draw up a life tenancy for May and Margaret Lucy. This may have seemed a good way for Pop to secure his wife and daughter's future but it caused great pressure on Cha and the family when Pop died and the life tenancy became a reality. There was little space for the growing family, as both living and sleeping quarters became overcrowded. This only added to the family's difficulties.

13. Portrait of Joe Carr in Portmarnock Golf Club

Raymond also filled me in on The Carr family. They had always had a fine standard of living, as Jim Carr received a pension from the army, as well as a salary from the golf club. When they went on a Mediterranean cruise in 1932, they took their 10-year old son with them. Sadly, on December 14 1939, Jim Carr died from heart failure, after a short illness. He was just 56 years old. Cha and Charlie were among the chief mourners at his funeral mass, held at Saints Peter and Paul Church, Baldoyle. The Costigans' connection with Portmarnock was now at an end. May subsequently returned to Rosslare Harbour and lived there for ten years. When Pop died in November 1949, May and her mother moved to Dublin to live with Cha and the McGovern family.

After Jim Carr's death, Kathleen and 17-year old Joe had to leave Pormarnock, as the position of steward was terminated. They moved in with two maiden aunts, sharing a single room over a shop in Emmet Road, Inchicore. It was a dramatic change in circumstances after all the luxury and grandeur of Portmarnock. The following years during World War II were hard for both of them but soon Joe got on his feet. He set his mother up in the fashion business and she kept this going, with the support of her son, until her death in 1972. Joe continued to have great success in business and in sport. He founded the *House of Carr* fashion business, from the mid-70s to the mid-80s, at one point employing a staff of 800. In golfing terms, he is considered to be the best Irish amateur player of all time. The little boy that Sue, Cha and May had so often babysat became a sporting legend of world renown.

BACK IN DUBLIN, FROM 1990

Over the following months I noticed subtle changes creeping into my life. I didn't worry as much about the future. My general spirits were lighter and not nearly as morose as I'd previously experienced. The reading with Brendan had given me much to think about. Most importantly, if reincarnation was a universal truth, then life had meaning built into it. I was intrigued and wanted to know more.

I began taking courses in The Irish Spiritual Centre, as the Irish Spiritual Movement was not called. One of my favourites was *The Light Within*. A previously unexplored world opened up for me. There were physical laws of impermanence that we were subject to in this world but, in spiritual terms, there were basic laws of cause and effect, synchronicity, attraction and ultimately the eternal nature of spirit that were the bedrock of the universe. I attended meditations at the centre and also began studying spiritual healing with the National Federation of Spiritual Healers. In parallel with these studies, I began training to become a psychotherapist, taking diploma courses in counselling, reality therapy, family therapy and hypnoanalysis. Later, I studied for a degree in psychology to have a thorough grounding in the whole area of healing and mental health.

Despite many disappointments along my path, I no longer felt lost or depressed. Slowly, I developed a more positive outlook, greater skills for dealing with emotional upheavals and a deeper understanding of the true nature of life. I began to enjoy the really simple things, such as the pleasure of a sunset, the tiny buds bursting forth in springtime, the play of light and shade when sitting in a park on a sunny day.

I went through a difficult time though when my relationship with Philo disintegrated, despite my best efforts to save it. Looking back, I feel he must have been manic depressive, with his constant change in moods from elation to blackest despair. His tendency to drink excessively only exacerbated his problems. We had several breakups and then reunited only to get back on the same emotional rollercoaster. Ultimately, he knew he needed to be alone to get his life back on track. I sorely missed his companionship, the great talks we used to have and all the excursions around the city that I loved so much. We had experienced moments of passion but the love I had hoped would ensue had never materialised. It was a tough lesson to learn that, despite having many ingredients in place, nothing can replace a mutual depth of love that is vital for a relationship to flourish. Still, I knew it would take me a long time to overcome the loss of this very special man who I had loved deeply.

This was also a time when I made some really good friends on the counselling course I took and in the spiritual centre. We attended workshops together, began socialising and slowly developed strong bonds, supporting each other through many tough times. These like-minded people were on similar paths of self-discovery and we are still good friends today.

All of this coincided with a newfound sense of freedom and fun. I had never been on a plane and yet in October 1990 I spent a month travelling around Thailand with my good friend, Carmel. We travelled from Bangkok to the northern territory of Chang Mai and then south to the paradise island of Koh Samui. We found ourselves in a country where reincarnation is an accepted fact. We visited many Buddhist temples, called wat, each beautifully decorated with flowers, candles, incense and statues encased in gold leaf. In Koh Samui we stayed for ten days in Big Buddha Beach. The statue of the golden Buddha dominated the island so, as the days slipped by, we just had to visit the temple that so many locals had told us about.

One afternoon, we walked the long flight of steps up to Big Buddha temple, called Wat Phra Yai. We entered a large courtyard that was surrounded by long buildings with ornate red roofs, rich mosaic columns, golden statues and decorative cornices. The place was eerily deserted but we walked around on the off-chance that someone would come out to us. Finally, a Buddhist monk in orange robes appeared and welcomed us to the temple. His English was very limited but he somehow communicated to us that we needed to meditate deeply on death, the decomposition of the body and the realisation that we will continue to be reborn until we reach Nirvana. He placed woven bracelets on our wrists and gave us both a blessing.

Carmel and I were both in our mid-20s, filled with a curiosity to explore and experience so much that this world might offer. Surrounded by the natural beauty of this exotic island, we were ill-prepared for dwelling on death. After the visit to the monk though, as I sat on the white sands and paddled in the warmth of the South China Sea, I did feel that something had been awakened in me, certainly not to waste today but to fully experience all the magnificence around me.

The following year found me in Hong Kong where Carmel was working on a three-month contract. The city of Hong Kong was so cosmopolitan that it inspired a great feeling of freedom and openness. This was followed by many travels around Europe with various friends, with my sister, Theresa and my nephew, Michael.

Spending time with my family in Wexford was always important to me. Theresa had three sons and Anthony had three daughters. A deep love and friendship permeated our close-knit circle. I became particularly close to my nephews, Michael and Paul, and to my niece, Sharon. Over the years, they often stayed with me in Dublin and we had marvellous fun, visiting landmarks around the city, going bowling and playing tennis in Bushy Park.

My parents were by this time elderly but I still loved their company. Dad developed a lot of problems with his eyes and sadly became blind. My Mam read newspapers and books to him and he had his beloved radio to listen to. I introduced Paddy

McMahon's series of books, *The Grand Design* to them. These were certainly a departure from the Catholic doctrine that my parents had been brought up with but at least they read and discussed them.

My aunt May sadly developed dementia. It began with forgetfulness, escalated to her becoming anxious and fearful, then culminated in her losing her grip on reality. In the early 1990s, her condition worsened and the family agreed that she needed to be looked after in a nursing home in Co. Wexford. It wasn't the ideal situation but May had regular visitors and seemed to take well to her new home.

I saw Brendan on a regular basis when I was studying in the centre. I brought him in the photo of Sue, Tom and Cha and filled him in on some of the details I had found out about her life. "It all fits then," he grinned. "I thought it might."

I recall one winter's day when I met him. I was wearing my long black coat that had a fur collar and I was wrapped up in a long velvet scarf. "That reminds me of you in your last life," he gestured to my attire. "That was the way you liked to dress then." I had never shown him the photo of Sue sitting in the garden in Rosslare Harbour, wearing a long black coat with fur cuffs and collar. His intuition and ability to access such information from other realms was uncanny.

Around this time I came across a book, *Yesterdays Children*, by a woman who had always felt that she had lived before. Jenny Cockell lived in Northamptonshire in England but she had memories and dreams of another life, as Mary, in an Irish village. Mary had lived many years before Jenny was born, and had died at the age of 21, leaving behind several young children who were subsequently motherless. Jenny felt great anxiety about these past-life memories and, as an adult, decided to search for 'her' lost children. By undergoing hypnosis, searching through maps and contacting local groups in Ireland, Jenny located the village where Mary had lived. Jenny finally made the trip to Malahide, Co. Dublin, found the house where she had lived as Mary and was ultimately reunited with her children.

This was the best case for verified evidence of a past life that I had ever come across. Looking through books and articles today, it is still very rare to find a person writing about their own story of a possible past life. Although every life story is unique, I couldn't help but compare Jenny's story to mine. Jenny had vivid memories and dreams of living as Mary, whereas for me, it had all unfolded at a more subtle level, with feelings and impressions guiding my choices and preferences, such as my overwhelming interest in the 1920s; my love of Dublin; my vegetarian diet and abhorrence of blood; my reluctance to stay indoors in the house where Sue had been ill during her final months. Also there was the recurring dream of white roses being put on a grave by a man in deep grief and my apprehension when approaching the age of 21. Any one of these feelings could easily be discounted but, when lined up together and placed alongside Brendan's reading, the combined experiences become very compelling.

It was Wednesday, July 28, 1993 when I went back to Brendan for another reading. It had been over three years since the previous one, when those revelations about a past life had surfaced. I wondered this time what was in store for me.

"You're a complicated person", Brendan began. "What I'm trying to do here is to sort out this question of your sister. Now, I know in your last incarnation you had a sister that is still alive in this life. It's that sister we are talking about now, your sister then but your aunt now who is in old-age. Your grandmother—your mother in your last life—is saying she's a bit crabby in her old age."

"She's in a home," I told him.

"Ok. She's become more aware of you lately. She's beginning to relate more to you as her sister again. And I wouldn't be a bit surprised if she mistook you for her then. It'll be interesting to see. So don't be surprised if she gets mixed-up, perhaps she'll call you by the wrong name or something. It should be very interesting to see how things are when she gets back to the other side and finds that you're here. I feel it'll be pretty good then for you because it'll be a more normal relationship than anything which exists at this present moment in time."

I nodded, trying to take it all in. Brendan continued.

"Your grandmother is going to restore the power balance in the family. I feel she's going to alter your position in relation to the family as well, because the family is beginning to look more to you for a sense of responsibility or guidance. She's wholly behind this work you're doing with regard to counselling. It's only because you have the capabilities that she can work with you in this way. When someone asks you a question, you'll know it's been inspired by granny and you can give the answer that's been inspired as well."

"She's got a lovely sense of humour," Brendan smiled. "She's actually a very pleasant person to deal with, but a bit sarcastic which takes a bit of getting used to. She's been away from the Wexford area for a while. I do feel that England is the place...she's working with someone. Does your father have a half-brother?"

"No, but I have an adopted brother," I said.

"And is he in England?"

I nodded.

"That's the one. It's as though he was trying to get things in order and she was giving him a helping hand. It's as though he has boxes of stuff and he seems to be packing. You know, if you were moving flat or something and you were trying to decide which box should go in the bin and which should go with you."

"He was moving house," I interjected.

"Yes, there's a lot of nostalgia in these boxes and I feel he was at quite an emotional level during it and this is where she was helping him to cope. The sort of thing I was looking at was him packing photographs and things into boxes and looking at them and trying to sort them out. You may have noticed the grandmother's absence then."

"The other thing is," Brendan continued, "that your grandmother is happy with the course you are pursuing. She would be quite a good analyst. In her past, she may have filled this role in some kind of way, being a bit of a sage. She'll be a very good ally in the area you're going to work in. This is all part of the change in your own sensitivity. She seems to be working very hard on that."

Brendan talked in detail about many aspects of my life during that reading. I still wondered how he could sense so much. He mentioned both my mam and dad, saying that my mam wasn't content as she felt a lot of responsibility was being thrust on her shoulders. This was probably true at a time when my Dad had gone blind and depended on her for everything. Brendan also said that my dad's energy felt as though "he's died and is in another world." That worried me but I hoped it was metaphorical.

With regard to my career, Brendan said, "I feel you're certainly going to work in the area where you're studying at this moment in time, and you're going to turn around and give the institution or establishment you're working with the two-fingered sign comparatively shortly. I would take you into this time next year or slightly later next year—so you've about 13 or 14 months perhaps before you'd be in a position to do something like that."

Afterwards, I felt kind of overwhelmed with the enormity of it all, hearing from a family member in spirit, my grandmother—Sue's mother—and being told that she was working with me on trying to restore power to our family. When I went home to visit, I mentioned to my parents that I had had a reading but I didn't give many details. It was all too much to handle. I visited my aunt May though in the home that was caring for her. She was agitated when I arrived with my mother and my nephew, Michael.

May was sitting on the bed, dressed in her hat and coat, searching through her bag.

"I'll be late if I don't hurry up," she said. "I've to go to work."

"Where do you have to go?" I asked.

"I've lots to do," she answered, still pulling things in and out of her bag. "I've to get to Portmarnock. I'll be late."

It took a long time to settle her down. Her strong work ethic in Portmarnock had somehow taken hold and she found herself back in those days, determined to resume her busy role there. Her mind had sadly deteriorated and she switched from one topic and reality to the next. It was difficult for all of us to see May so disorientated.

The remainder of the reading would become truly significant, beginning six months later. On January 17, 1994 my Dad passed away, just a few weeks short of his eightieth birthday. Our little family unit was devastated. Later, my sister confided that she had been awoken several nights before my dad's passing by the vision of our grandmother in her bedroom. She had felt very afraid and had pulled the covers over her head, hoping whatever it was would go away. Although a major shock, I could only feel the vision had been a message, offering a little time to Theresa to prepare for Dad's imminent departure. I felt my Dad's loss greatly but I was truly glad I had had that reading with Brendan and had learned that our grandmother, Margaret Lucy–Sue's mother–was working with me and all of the family.

After over 40 years of loving this very special man, my mother couldn't continue alone. She developed serious health issues and followed him to the spirit world on January 20 the following year. I was shaken to the core to lose my parents who were also my best friends. I kept visualising them surrounded by light, at last free from the physical discomforts of life and embarking on new, exciting pursuits. This helped me to allow them to pass on, with much love and gratitude, for all they had given me in this life.

Back in the spiritual centre, Brendan asked me to become the counsellor there as many people who came for healing were also in need of counselling. I was delighted to be given this great opportunity, though also a little nervous. I took the plunge and really enjoyed my years there, working at nights and some weekends, learning so much from the many brave and beautiful people I had the privilege to work with.

I still kept in contact with my cousin Raymond. On Saturday, September 17 1994, we met in Rathmines to spend the day retracing the steps of our ancestors, on a walking tour of the Liberty's and Dublin South West. We walked westwards, taking in Cork Street, the Coombe, Basin Lane, James Street, Bow Lane, Old Kilmainham, Bully's Acre, Liffey Street South, East Square, the Inchicore Railway Works, Tyrconnell Park and the Oblates church and graveyard, located in Tyrconnell Road, Inchicore. It was evening by the time we arrived at Ray's home in Jamestown, Inchicore.

The one really surreal event that day was when we stood outside of 16 East Square, Inchicore, the former home of our great-aunts, Cha Deegan and

Eileen Flynn, Cha Deegan's daughters, Annie and Cha, and our great-grand father, Michael Flynn. I had met Annie several times when I visited her home as a child with May. I remember her playing the beautiful *Für Elise* by Beethoven on the piano. As we stood outside the house where our families had experienced so many milestones in their lives, the haunting melody of *Für Elise* enveloped us. An ice cream van had turned into the square and proceeded to play this tune. Coincidence, synchronicity or otherwise, it was a spine-tingling moment.

Around this time, Raymond presented me with an old book that had been passed down through the family over generations. It was *The Sinner's Guide*, by Fr. Lewis of Granada, written in 1555. This was the book that Sue had been reading in the old photograph that Ray had given to me. In the photo, Sue is sitting, wearing a cloche hat, wrapped up in a fur-collared coat, outside her home in Rosslare Harbour, towards the end of her life. The book is inscribed by various people, some of them family members. Sue had written her name twice towards the beginning of the book. It is a difficult book to read, with the letter 'f' replacing 's' all through the text. It is a book of Christian doctrine: how to lead a virtuous life, to insure that you are raised up to heaven and how to avoid the pitfalls that could lead to hell and damnation. I imagine it was a very sobering book for a seriously ill 20-year old to be reading. The passages I read certainly failed to provide me with a positive vision of life as an everlasting journey, into the light of growing awareness.

Susanah Costigan

THE
ARGUMENT to the FIRST BOOK.

1. THIS firſt book, Chriſtian Reader, contains an ample exhortation to virtue, that is, to the keeping of God's commandments, wherein true virtue confiſts. It is divided into three principal parts. The firſt is a perſuaſive to virtue, to this purpoſe making uſe of all thoſe arguments holy authors for the moſt part have brought upon this ſubjeċt, which are our infinite obligations to Almighty God, as well in regard of what he is in himſelf as what he is to us, on account of his ineſtimable benefits, as alſo of what great conſequence virtue itſelf is to us, which is ſufficiently made out by man's four laſt things, death, judgment, hell and heaven, which is the ſubjeċt of this firſt part.

2. The ſecond is to perſuade the ſame thing, but by other arguments, viz. The advantages of grace promiſed to virtue in this life; and here are ſet down twelve ſingular privileges belonging to it, every one of which is particularly diſcourſed of. Though holy authors ſometimes briefly hint at theſe privileges, ſpeaking of the peace, inward light, true liberty, comfort of a good conſcience, and conſolations of the Holy Ghoſt, enjoyed by the juſt, and the uſual concomitants of virtue, yet I have not met with any body that has handled this ſubjeċt at large and in due order. This has put me to ſome more labour in picking out and putting together all theſe matters out of ſeveral parts of the holy ſcriptures, giving them their proper names, placing them in order, and expounding and backing them with ſeveral other texts of ſcripture, and of the

writings

14. Sue Costigan's signature on 'A Sinner's Guide'

115

My mind returned to my childhood visits to Dad's family home in Rosslare Harbour. I could still remember the feeling of stuffiness in the house and my need to get outside. Perhaps this was a memory of how Sue had felt, desperately wanting to sit out in the sun in the garden, a short reprieve from lying alone in her sickbed.

In the mid-90s I became focused again on my dream of becoming a writer. I sent in a thesis I had completed for women's studies on complementary therapies to Wolfhound Press. It was miraculous that the manuscript was accepted and my first book, *Irish Guide to Complementary and Alternative Therapies* was published in 1996.

My life as a computer programmer for the financial institution I had worked in for a decade began to rapidly fall apart. I joined a union and became involved in looking for better conditions. Suffice it to say that this move was not welcomed by management and I found myself being ostracised and singled-out for unfair treatment. Luckily, in October 1997, with the help of Frank, a marvellously kind and astute union representative, I received a redundancy package and I was finally free to move on with my life and my new career. It may have taken a few years longer than Brendan had predicted in my reading but at last it had come to pass.

WEXFORD AND BEYOND, FROM 1997

The sense of freedom I felt at leaving the job I had long outgrown was overwhelming. I moved back to Wexford to the family home that my parents had kindly left me. I began to take clients for counselling and hypnotherapy. I also started writing again and my second book, *Bullying and Harassment in the Workplace* was published by Columba Press in 1998.

After all the stress I'd experienced in my final months at work, I developed sciatica and discovered that I had a slipped disc. This required many months of rest and healing. Perhaps as an antidote to this inactivity, I decided to start a local magazine, *Wexford Life*, helped and actively aided by the other members of my family, including our cousin, Raymond. In many ways, the magazine showcased each member's skills: Anthony was the illustrator, music critic and contributor; Theresa was our researcher; Michael, my nephew, was the photographer; Raymond was in charge of advertising and was also a major contributor. Our teenage members, Paul and Sharon, had their own column. We stayed in business for two years, bringing out a final edition for the millennium.

I often thought about Sue during those years. She was in a different time when opportunities were limited but there was still no knowing what she could have achieved if she had lived a full life. I often felt her energy with me, encouraging me to face my fears and to go for it, to open to new experiences that resonated with my soul.

There was no sadness anymore when I thought of Sue. I felt I had a better understanding of why, at a soul level, she might have needed to leave this life to review her plans and, at a later stage, return to give life another try. I still often contemplated if Sue and I were made of the same soul fabric, for want of a better term. Initially, I may have felt burdened by the assertion that I was Sue's reincarnation. It made me feel responsible in some way for making sure that my life wasn't wasted or unfulfilled since I could have been carrying the can for Sue and me. Whatever I had come here to accomplish I needed to do it, so that our soul could progress. That was a strange kind of responsibility to carry but there it was: I didn't want to disappoint Sue or to let her down in any way.

One thing was for sure: My life wouldn't have unfolded in the same way if I hadn't gone for that reading in March 1990, met Brendan O'Callaghan and discovered the true connection with my aunt, Sue. Before I began to learn about spirituality, I was like a leaf being blown by the wind. I was at sea, rudderless. Not only the readings but the many workshops and meditations I attended at the Spiritual Centre, gave me greater clarity as to the true nature of life and the role that I could play in the world, through my work and my writing.

Most of the time though I just got on with life, struggling to make the right decisions to propel myself forward. In October 2000, I was given the opportunity—literally out of the blue—to take on a contract in technical writing in Silicon Valley, California. I had never worked in this area before and I had just started studying for a master's degree in equality studies in Dublin. I was very reluctant to work abroad and, indeed, daunted by the prospect. I grappled with doubts and fears but finally decided to give it a go.

This opportunity led to spending three amazing years in Santa Clara with Bob, the work colleague I met on my first day there, who became my partner and dear friend. For the three years we were together we travelled all over California and into Nevada, visiting Texas and Utah, spending Christmas of 2002 on the east coast, exploring so many states, each with its own magic and beauty. It was also a time when I attended Buddhist meditations in Redwood, California, became a regular attendee at spiritual seminars in East West in Mountain View, and was immersed in the culture and spiritual teachings of the most enlightened American Indian tribes. I was most drawn to the Hopi tradition, from north-eastern Arizona, with their reverence and respect for all things, their desire for peace and to live according to the guidance of the Creator.

I remember one hot Saturday in the middle of summer when we came across the Ryde Hotel in Walnut Grove, located on the banks of the Sacramento River. It had been built in 1927 at the peak of the prohibition era in the US. It was an opulent establishment, its lower level having been a speakeasy in the 1920s, offering bootleg whiskey and jazz to a clientele in search of a good time. There was even a trap door in the floor that allegedly opened to reveal a tunnel running under the road that led to a hidden doorway at the river's edge. It had been the favoured haunt of movie stars, politicians and mobsters. I thought back to Sue then and to the simple elegance of the Portmarnock Golf Club that May had often referred to. In the same year that Sue began waitressing in the club, the bawdy and glitzy Ryde Hotel in California was opening its doors to a very different clientele.

One year, for Bob's birthday, we travelled down south to San Simeon, located in the central coast of California, to visit Hearst Castle. The design of the castle was developed by the publisher and multi-millionaire, William Randolph Hearst, and his architect Julia Morgan. It was famous for its lavish parties in the 1920s and 30s that was attended by Hollywood guests, such as Greta Garbo and Clark Gable. We took the tour of the castle that showcased the magnificent antiques, furniture, statues, ornate swimming pools, home theatre and sumptuous guest rooms. It was just the way I had imagined Gatsby's mansion to be designed, in that era of decadence and excess.

I still managed to travel home fairly regularly. I somehow completed the equality studies course and took on another master's degree in research. I missed my family so much when I was in California that I couldn't stay away for very long. This was also a time when we lost some of our closest relatives. My Uncle Joe left this world on November 9, 2000, aged 84. His wife, May, had already been many years deceased, having passed on June 15, 1994, aged 81. The last of the clan, my Aunt May, had out-lived all of her siblings. May passed over on May 18, 2001, aged 94. The original cast that had played such a vital role in Sue's short life, and in my entire life so far, had finally crossed over.

FURTHER READINGS

I arrived back in Ireland on the last day of January, 2004. Bob and I had come to a crossroads: Either marry and live in California or split-up and I would return to Ireland. For months we teetered on the brink of marriage. When you care immensely for someone and become familiar with the day to day life that you share, it is all too easy to cover up the cracks, the lack of passion and true compatibility, and try to pretend that the relationship is something it isn't. I was very sad and lonely to leave Santa Clara, missing Bob and the friendship we had shared, and trying to figure out how I would begin again in Wexford.

I immediately set about planting roots by decorating my home that had been largely vacant for three years, setting up a counselling and psychotherapy business in the town and taking on part-time work in a local resource centre, working with people with disabilities. Over the years I have found a niche there, developing programmes for wellness, positive living and relaxation. I also felt a great contentment to be back with my family, where I felt I truly belonged.

In June 2004, Raymond phoned to tell me that Joe Carr had passed from this world on June 3, at the age of 82. Although Joe had practised golf in

Portmarnock as a child, he wasn't welcomed as a member of the club due to his father being steward there, so he began playing in Sutton Golf Club. It was here that he achieved outstanding success, winning three British amateur titles, 37 national and provincial titles, making 11 appearances in the Walker Cup and being given the Bob Jones Award for outstanding sportsmanship in golf by the US Golf Association: The first time a non-American citizen ever received the award. He was subsequently elected to the World Golf Hall of Fame in 2007.

When the banking crisis erupted in 2008, it coincided with my desire to cease working with clients. To be honest, it was probably a case of burnout. I had been a therapist for almost 15 years and I really felt I needed a break from focusing so completely on other people's struggles. I had probably lost myself in the role of counsellor, being available to family, friends and acquaintances 24-7 as listener, empathiser and mentor. Maybe this was a way of not having to look at my own needs and inadequacies, by focusing instead on others' problems. For my own wellbeing, it was something I had to change.

I was happy though to continue my part-time work in social care and I also began to devote more time to writing. This was the start of a very creative and fulfilling time that all of my family, including Raymond, had a role in. I began to research the stained-glass windows of Harry Clarke as I had always had a passion for his work. This led to *Strangest Genius: The stained glass of Harry Clarke*, a book that catalogued his entire collection worldwide. Michael, my nephew, did the photography and it was published by The History Press in 2010. Michael also set up a website for Clarke's work and we also made our first documentary on Clarke, *A Revel in Blue*, directed by my brother, Anthony.

We also established our own publishing firm, Enlighten Publishing in 2014 and published our first book, *Winter Solstice: A Novel*, set in Newgrange on the morning of the winter solstice. We each seemed to be bursting with ideas for books, films and even a play that we began writing, entitled, *The Last Day of Harry Clarke*.

I often thought of the readings I had had with Brendan, in the early 1990's, that had jolted me into a new and very unfamiliar world. Since then, there have been a few times over the intervening years when I have looked for guidance from other spiritual mediums. In the summer of 2014, I was doing a lot of soul-searching. I was looking for direction again in many areas of my life.

In May 2014, I had a short reading with Linda Shalloe, a wonderful healer and angel reader in Co. Wexford. When she inquired at the end of the reading if I had any questions, I asked if she could pick up anything about a past life. She said that my last life had been in Edwardian times. This was certainly close to Sue's birth in 1911 as Edwardian referred to Edward VII's reign from 1901 to 1910. Linda continued, saying she could feel that I had been constricted in some way and hadn't been allowed to speak up in that life. She said there had been a constriction of my breathing as though I couldn't express myself then. Constriction was a very apt word for the breathing problems Sue must have experienced as she struggled to deal with the onset of TB. It could also be applied to Sue's upbringing which, in the early 1900s in Ireland, must have been very constricting for a young girl, under the harsh restrictions of school but also at home, imposed by an overly-religious mother.

Linda suggested that one of the reasons I came back into this life was to express myself through writing. This really resonated with me as, even in this life, I have often felt it difficult to speak my own truth for fear of ridicule or rejection. I know this is why I have written since I was a child, to express my feelings and experiences boldly, using a medium where I feel comfortable.

Then Clara, a good friend and colleague from my days in the Spiritual Centre in Dublin, contacted me, saying that Brendan was doing readings again after a long layoff. She had already booked in for one in June. I asked her to book me in too. So, on Friday, June 27th 2014, I found myself once again opening to the spirit world while sitting for a reading with Brendan. I hadn't seen Brendan for at least a decade and it had been 24 years since my initial reading. I wondered if there would be any further revelations about my past life in the height of the 1920s. In particular, I wanted to know what Brendan had meant all those years ago by saying that Sue had 'gone off track'. As the reading progressed, nothing was emerging about that life so I asked Brendan if there was anything else from that previous life that I needed to know about.

I was more than a little disappointed that nothing new emerged. Brendan described a scene that he could clearly see, a wardrobe that was filled with many types of clothing. For each lifetime, he told me, we choose a body, just like changing into a new set of clothes. This is a necessary disguise, he said, for the lessons we need to learn while here on earth. He again reiterated that the lessons I had avoided learning in my previous life had led me into this incarnation. He clearly stated, just as he had done in March 1990, that I had encountered some tough situations in this life that had given me the opportunity to learn the required lessons and to develop spiritually. That was all, he said, that was being channelled about my past life.

Afterwards, I felt that the need for readings had passed and that I no longer needed confirmation that I had lived in the 1920s as Susanah Frances Costigan. There had been so many coincidences—or signposts—since I was a child that connected our lives and drew them ever closer. I clearly had to admit that there was some special bond that linked us. For many years now there had been no dreams of roses or graves or sadness. I felt happy enough to leave the past alone and to get on with today's living, as one life seemed more than enough to handle.

15. Raymond McGovern and I, June 2, 2011

REGRESSION

It was in the spring of 2015 that I met an old friend for coffee and a chat. He mentioned that he had booked a ticket to attend a workshop on regression. It was to take place in the Clyde Hotel in Dublin, the following month, and the host for the night was Dr. Brian Weiss. I certainly perked up when I heard that the illustrious regressionist would be conducting a workshop in Dublin. It reminded me of an evening when I had stayed with my friend Clara in Dublin and, knowing I loved to read, she had left a book on the bedside table that she felt I'd be interested in. It was entitled *Only Love Is Real: A Story of Soulmates Reunited* (1997) by Dr. Brian Weiss. Several hours late into the night I was still reading. I couldn't put it down. I couldn't wait to find out if the two soulmates depicted would finally be reunited. The next day I bought a copy as I wanted to reread it, slowly, along with Dr. Weiss' first book, *Many Lives, Many Masters: The True Story of a Prominent Psychiatrist, His Young Patient, and the Past-Life Therapy That Changed Both Their Lives* (1988).

Dr. Weiss really interested me because for many years he had been a very traditional psychiatrist, being promoted to Chairman Emeritus of Psychiatry at the Mount Sinai Medical Centre in Miami. Dr. Weiss had no belief in reincarnation or past lives at that time. By his own account, he was amazed but very sceptical when one of his patients, Catherine, began to describe past life experiences under hypnosis that ultimately led to her complete recovery, from recurring nightmares and bouts of anxiety. His scepticism was eroded when Catherine began to channel messages from "the space between lives", which contained remarkable revelations about Dr. Weiss's family and his dead son. Dr. Weiss then became an advocate of past-life therapy, working with thousands of people through regression into past lives. For many years though he tried to conceal his therapeutic work into past lives for fear of ridicule from his colleagues. From my work and studies, I knew all about the professional rules of conduct for hypnotherapists and psychoanalysts that disallowed them from delving into clients' past lives. I really admired Dr. Weiss' efforts to bring his client's experiences of past lives into the full glare of the psychiatric realm.

According to Dr. Weiss, people experience past lives, not just in hypnosis, but also in dreams or déjà vu experiences, for example, when a person is travelling in an unfamiliar place and uncannily knows their way around. Past lives can also be sparked off by meeting someone and feeling that you've known them for years.

I had never experienced past life regression before, although I had regularly practiced self-hypnosis and had also attended for my own hypnoanalysis, as part of my clinical training. I wondered if, through regression, I could find the answer to why Sue had to die so young when everything seemed to be going so well for her. I was still pondering why Brendan had said that Sue had

129

gone off track. How could that happen, I mused? Had she done something that steered her so off course that she had to exit that life? I decided to buy a ticket and to accompany my friend to the event.

We were almost the first to arrive that evening in the Clyde Hotel so we chose seats in the front row. The room was soon buzzing as other participants took their seats. There was definitely an air of anticipation. Dr. Weiss finally came out and sat on the low stage, right in front of me. He was softly spoken and considerate, wanting everyone to have a good experience.

From the notes I wrote down after the event, the following is a close depiction of the way the regression unfolded. Dr. Weiss began by asking us to get comfortable in our chairs, as the session would last around 25 to 30 minutes. Gentle music began playing in the background. He urged us to let whatever images, thoughts, feelings or sensations that came up for us during the session, to remain without analysis or criticism, while we were going through the experience. He also said that if anyone felt uncomfortable, they could open their eyes at any time. He then asked us to close our eyes.

As Dr. Weiss talked in his soft, gentle voice, I became deeply relaxed. Once I closed my eyes I was oblivious to everyone else in the room. Even the excitement, mixed with a tinge of anxiety about being there, began to fade. He urged us to use our imaginations, to breathe in relaxing energy, then to breathe out and to let go of all our stresses.

He then asked us to slowly release tension from all parts of our body; to relax each of our muscles, beginning with the head and face, moving down to the neck and shoulders, the stomach and abdomen, the back, arms, legs and feet. Then he asked us to visualise a beautiful light that was bringing healing to all parts of the body, moving in through the top of the head, illuminating the brain and spinal cord. The light continued to flow down like a beautiful wave of energy, touching every cell of the body, every fibre, every tissue and every organ, bringing peace, love and healing.

I felt myself begin to relax deeply, lulled by the sound of his voice and fully focused on imaging the beautiful light bringing healing to every part of me. Dr. Weiss began to count down from 10 to 1, urging us to go deeper, so that we could remember every experience that we had ever had, either in this life, in other lives or when we were in-between physical lives, in the spiritual realm. Then he began to count down slowly, urging us to go deeper and deeper into relaxation and peace.

When he reached number 1, he asked us to visualise a beautiful garden, a sanctuary that was filled with exquisite flowers and trees, and surrounded by light. Then he began counting down again, this time from 5 to 1, suggesting that we would recall a childhood memory when he reached 1. He asked that we pay attention to any details that emerged and to allow the memories to surface. He also reassured us that at any time, if we felt anxious, we could float about the scene and go back to the beautiful garden, or open our eyes.

I took a deep breath and felt myself relax even deeper. A memory immediately flashed into my mind. I was walking towards Redmond's Park in Wexford Town with a group of friends, on our way to visit their relatives. I was about 8 years old. It was a lovely sunny afternoon. I hadn't thought of this memory in decades. I felt light and happy. We called to a house with a lovely front garden. We went inside and sat around a big table where we were given the most beautiful brown bread and jam by a kindly old lady. There were feelings of great freedom and happiness.

Dr. Weiss was speaking again, asking us to float above the memory now, feeling a great sense of freedom and lightness. He asked us to ponder why that particular memory came up for us, out of the thousands of memories we could have recalled.

I figured this was to do with the lonely times I spent as a child, not having many friends. This memory showed me how happy I felt when I was treated well and felt that I belonged.

After a few moments, he urged us to go further back in time, when we were in utero in our mother's womb. This time, he counted from 5 to 1. He asked how we felt about our parents, about any lessons we were here to learn.

I felt warm and wrapped in love and goodness. I knew my mother loved me and also my father. I felt some of her anxiety though that she might lose me. I saw her reading and felt happy that she was absorbed in her book. If there was any lesson, it was that love is the greatest gift of all. I was aware again of his voice, asking that we go through our birth, with no pain or discomfort. I felt love and great relief.

This time Dr. Weiss asked us to float above the scene and to prepare to go back further, perhaps into a past life. He said there was a doorway and that on the other side of the door there was a beautiful light. When the door opened, we could see the light and, beyond the light, there would be a scene from a past life. He counted down once again, from 5 to 1. He asked us to look down and to see what we were wearing on our feet, what our clothes looked like, if we could see any buildings or landscape, or if we recognised anyone.

My door opened and I was met by a guide. I was running along the seashore, aged maybe 7 or 8. I had bare legs. I kept on running, so delighted to be free in the sunshine. There were other children running after me. They were my friends. The feeling of freedom and happiness continued. I was very fit and agile. I could run very fast. I was delighted to be alive.

Then the scene switched to an open area beside a different sea and I was walking on a promenade. I was meeting my love there. I was wearing boots and a long dark red coat with fur at the cuffs and collar. I felt so excited and happy. I was full of love for this man who looked so smart beside me. We were very much in love.

The scene switched and we were on his motorcycle. We were riding very fast along the promenade. I held him tight. I loved the view of the sea whizzing by and the feeling of freedom. We went down to the beach and had a picnic and a cuddle. We talked about our future plans. I couldn't stop laughing and smiling. I was so happy.

Then the scene changed again and we were walking together. I felt such love and joy. He was there with me and we kissed. I felt great excitement and love. We walked hand in hand along a road. There was a low stone wall to the right. I was beside the wall. I could see the beach and the sea to the right. It was a summer's evening. I was wearing a mid-length dress and low-heeled sandals. I kept holding on to my little hat. I couldn't stop laughing.

There was another change of scene and I was dancing some dance that had a lot of steps, like the Charleston. This was great fun. I knew all the steps off by heart. I was wearing a dark red beaded dress. I was ecstatic with happiness and I laughed a lot. I was dancing with my boyfriend.

Then the scene changed again and I was waiting to be collected from hospital. I was very impatient. My throat was sore and I kept sipping water. Suddenly, my man appeared and all was right with the world again as we hugged and held hands.

Dr. Weiss interjected, saying that in a few moments, when he counted from 3 to 1, we would visit the most significant event in that life.

Immediately, I found myself in a darkened room. I felt ill and weak. I couldn't believe how everything had changed. I still kept hoping that it would all come right. I felt so lonely and there was huge sadness. Everything I wanted had been lost.

Dr. Weiss was speaking again, saying he was about to count from 3 to 1. When he reached 1, we were to find ourselves at the end of that lifetime, feeling no pain or discomfort.

I still felt a deep sadness. My parents were with me. I couldn't breathe. My mother was wiping my brow. I was slipping away into a deep sleep. There was relief and peace when I had left my body.

I became aware once again of Dr. Weiss' gentle voice, asking us to float above the scene. He asked us to imagine that we were in a beautiful place, full of peace and light, and that a very beautiful, wise spiritual being, like a guide or a loved one, was beside us. We could ask this guide anything, to help us understand any aspect of our past life or anything else we still needed to know.

My guide told me that this wasn't the right path for me—for Sue, to be a wife and mother at that time because there was a plan to become a teacher and it hadn't happened. He told me it wasn't my—or Sue's—fault; it was just the wrong time. He said I am a teacher and healer in this life and I can do both through my writing. He said not to focus on my weaknesses, as I often do, as these are the thoughts that hold me back. He urged me to focus on my strengths, such as my writing. Then he assured me that the wisdom I hold will flow out into the world and will bring about change.

Then I asked my guide about the man who I had recently met and felt a lot of love for. My guide said I needed to feel what is between us. I tuned into this and it was a similar feeling as I had had in the previous lifetime, of love and deep connection. My guide reassured me that in this lifetime I will find mutual love and that it will last.

I was aware again of Dr. Weiss speaking, saying it was time to return to full waking consciousness, but reiterating that we would remember everything we had experienced. He told us that we were entering our body that we had left behind in the garden and that each of us would feel ourselves back in our bodies, fully grounded. He then counted one last time from 1 to 10, making sure we were coming back to an alert and wakeful state.

Outside, I said goodbye to my friend, glad to be out in the evening air. I walked the short distance to my hotel, thoughts and feelings whizzing around inside me. It had been over seven years since I had worked with anyone using hypnoanalysis. In all my years of using visualisation and meditation for my own self-development and relaxation, I had never experienced anything like I did that evening. It had all felt so real. The sense of freedom, happiness and love had made me giddy, yet the sadness and despair had left me depleted and drained. I felt exhausted but also deeply thankful to have had such an experience.

I certainly had a lot to ponder. The guide's intervention certainly gave me more insights into the reason why Sue's soul may have needed to exit that life so early. I felt relieved that I was finally on the right path. I knew I had lots more work to do but that was ok. In many ways, I relished the challenge.

In the following days, I felt a mixture of feelings, lightness at times but also sadness for a life not realised. I reminded myself that I was very much alive now with much to learn and accomplish. There was one memory that had surfaced during the regression that felt so familiar. It was the walk along the strand road with my boyfriend, with the stone wall to my right, overlooking the expanse of sea. I browsed through old photos on the internet and found one with the very same type of wall. It was Baldoyle Estuary in the early 1900s where a tide mill had been located, a water mill that was driven by the tides. I looked up the location on google maps. The walk from Tom's home in Sutton, to Strand Road, Baldoyle, is only six minutes. Continuing along this coastal route leads to Strand Road, Portmarnock, and ultimately to the Portmarnock Golf Club, a one hour and 14 minute walk from Tom's home. No wonder he bought a motorbike for travelling that distance every day to work. There's little doubt that on summer evenings it must have been intoxicating for Sue and Tom to saunter along that road, with the wind and the sea spray in their hair, feeling so carefree and in the throes of love.

I had a sense too that Brendan's reference to Sue having 'gone off track' had to do with the unique mission she had taken on before incarnating in her earth life. I suppose, no one ever knows the mission or purpose of any individual life. It is a reminder that we need to be less judgemental about other people as we really have no idea what they may be working through or learning in this lifetime. If Sue's soul felt it was time for her to return to spirit then that was the only outcome. Then she could wait, perhaps develop further in spirit, and prepare to make another attempt on earth to achieve her goal.

Then another memory surfaced, one from this life. It was walking in the opposite direction to the one that I felt sure that Sue and Tom had walked towards Portmarnock. I was with Philo, walking long

Clontarf road all the way into the city, the sea and the wind providing a cool balm on a hot summer's afternoon. I wondered if I was in some kind of time warp. The regression had left me feeling depleted and tired, yet it had been a fascinating experience. I jotted down as many notes as I could each night before falling into bed. I just needed lots of sleep before I was ready to make the transition back to the twenty-first century.

16. Old Tide Mill, Baldoyle Estuary, early 1900s

17. Tony Walsh and I at book launch of 'Understanding Suicide', July 2015

140

LIFE AND DEATH

Since that initial reading with Brendan in March 1990, I was opened, not only to the concept of past lives, but to the whole world of spirituality. I have asked many questions and sought countless answers since, trying to understand what this life is really about. After spending this morning doing all the normal daily chores, making breakfast, feeding my two King Charles spaniels, putting on washing and then hanging out a line of clothes, I may well ask, what is the meaning of life? At times it is difficult for me to accept that I lived a life as Sue in the 1920s, yet the experience of unearthing so much about our connection, gives me a greater sense of the continuity of life. The eternal nature of life isn't a belief any more, as it was when I was a child brought up in the Christian tradition. It is much more tangible than that. Certainly, I have much less fear of death, though the irony is that I really enjoy living now, aware of the many possibilities that every day presents.

In August 2015, I was enjoying a break in Glendalough, Co. Wicklow, after researching and writing the book, *Understanding suicide*, with Anthony Walsh, a very special man I had met when working on *Glenveagh Mystery*. It was the first morning of that holiday when I detected a lump just under my stomach. I went through a period of weeks when tests were being done and I didn't know what the outcome would be. I didn't want to die but I didn't feel great panic. All around that time I felt my mother's gentle presence, bringing me love and comfort. I even miraculously found footage from a British Pathe newsreel on youtube, of my mother being presented to President Douglas Hyde after her school had won the Drama League cup, on March 31 1939. I really felt this was her way of reaching out to me, connecting from the other side. I was also very fortunate to have Tony's support during this time. Not only did I have medical tests to deal with but there were also interviews and talks to attend based on our new book, an exploration of the social causes of suicide.

Before the operation, when I was lying there awaiting the anaesthetic, I accepted whatever the outcome would be, whether awakening in my hospital bed, continuing the experiences and the struggles here on earth, or floating into another realm, where I would be reunited with that large family that Brendan had spoken about, during my first reading.

Over the years I have read many books, watched films and interviews, listened to countless audios and attended workshops given by some of the leading lights in spiritual development. I have found *The Grand Design* series of books and *There are no goodbyes,* by the late Paddy McMahon, to be profoundly healing and insightful, with their clear explanations as to the reasons why a spirit might choose an earth life, as well as being a comprehensive exploration of the spirit world. The first volume of *The Grand Design* was one of two books, the other being *The Prophet* by Kahlil Gibran, which I read and reread after my dad's passing. Also, Deepak Chopra's teachings and meditations on opening to all the possibilities that an earth life can provide, offer a rich blend of spiritual and psychological insights. Then there is Eckhart Tolle, who makes such a strong case for the rewards of living in the moment and paying attention to what is here and now.

There is no subject more riveting than the nature of life and the inevitability of death. Each of us is born and will someday die, so whether or not life continues after death is of utmost importance to the vast majority of us. Many may refuse to face this fact, choosing instead avoidance or partial denial. There is no doubt that the body dies as the physical laws of temporal existence and impermanence are irrefutable. It is the spiritual laws that we need to ponder: the law of karma—of cause and effect—and above all, the eternal nature of life.

It is unfortunately often the case that we are most receptive to spirituality, to opening to the spiritual core of ourselves, when we are suffering. This awakening may be caused by physical, emotional or psychic pain, perhaps some profound loss or when a choice we have made has led to a difficult life situation. Sometimes it takes divine intervention to nudge us into an awareness of our spiritual nature. This happens when there is a miracle, when the physical laws are altered and the usual progression of events, such as an acute illness, is halted or reversed. There are also times when we witness some great phenomenon that the physical world fails to explain.

That day in March 1990, when I went for the spiritual reading with Brendan, there was a guiding hand that seemed to nudge me forwards, towards a path that really suited me at a soul level. I have often felt supported and, on a handful of occasions, delivered from potentially disastrous situations. It was reassuring to feel that my ancestors were accompanying me on the journey and, I'm certain, throwing in a helping hand when I asked for their guidance.

Whenever I share the experience of going for readings with acquaintances, I can understand their scepticism and their view that communication with the spirit realm is highly unlikely. Yet, all the major religions accept the existence of angels, where their role is one of messenger and intermediary, between the earth and the spirit world. Also, religious teachings profess that sacred books for millennia have been channelled through wise beings or prophets, who received visions and messages from God in dreams or heightened states of awareness. So much of the information I received from Brendan, and a handful of other mediums I have attended over the years, has been uncannily accurate. It is interesting to put these readings in the context of religious prophesy which is accepted by millions as being a valid form of communication with the spirit world.

While spirituality is all-encompassing and not the domain of any one religion, there are teachings within each religion that may bring greater awareness and enlightenment to its advocates. I began researching religious views on life after death for a documentary film that I was co-writing with Lugh Films, an Irish film company. All the major religions advocate the continuation of life after death. Religions differ in terms of the nature and structure of the afterlife. Christian, Islamic and adherents of Judaism believe that people live on earth once and that when they die there will be a process of judgement. Buddhism and Hinduism proffer that people do not live and die once, but are reincarnated a number of times and live a series of lives before reaching enlightenment.

In the west, rebirth is still an alien concept as it is not the doctrine of Christian religions. If rebirth had been a concept that I had grown up with I don't doubt that I would have had no problem in accepting that I was the reincarnation of Sue. In Asia, the concepts of rebirth and the law of karma are part of Hinduism and Buddhism. The law of karma explains why people are reborn on earth. Karma means 'action', and refers to a person's behaviour but also takes account of the way a person has lived his or her whole life. Both Buddhism and Hinduism teach that worldly pleasures are limited as to the amount of happiness they can bring, and that ultimately, a person will desire 'higher' or spiritual forms of fulfilment.

We may wonder who sets this whole process of reincarnation in motion. Eastern religions state that it is the person's own soul that determines whether or not a person is reborn. Rebirth occurs because of the law of karma which is a natural process that is central to the soul's make-up.

I was fascinated to see the extent that the information that had been channelled to both Brendan and to Paddy McMahon had dovetailed so well with the teachings of eastern religions. Hindus believe that people remain on the cycle of samsara (birth, death and rebirth), until they awaken to their true divine nature. For Buddhists, death is not the end of life. It is merely the end of the body we inhabit in this life and the next task is for the spirit that remains to seek out a new body. The location and family that a person is born into is the result of past deeds and experiences, and the accumulation of positive and negative actions or karma.

The supreme aim of Buddhism is to obtain nirvana, meaning 'a state of liberation' or illumination from the limitations of existence. Nirvana is a state that is obtainable in this life through right aspirations, purity of mind and the elimination of the ego. Then a person will no longer mistakenly believe that he or she is above anyone else. These teachings are very close to those detailed in *The Grand Design* series by Paddy McMahon.

When going about our daily lives, it is easy to lose sight of the bigger picture. But it is in these tiny moments that we may take a giant step by becoming aware of the profound influence we have on every person we ever meet. It is so easy to judge and to let our respect slip but we really have no idea why a person is here on earth or what qualities they may be trying to develop in this lifetime. A word of encouragement may light up the world of another in ways we may never know. There is always so much more to learn and to experience. It seems we are on an eternal journey of discovery, growing in awareness, empathy and compassion.

Even in the world of science that has traditionally been opposed to all religious or spiritual teachings, scientists are proposing theories as to the continuation of life. This essence or core of life, referred to as consciousness, is defined as the part of any lifeform that is aware and responsive to stimuli and experiences. There are some fascinating developments in the world of science that are beginning to converge with spiritual wisdom as to the nature of consciousness. The law of physics states that nothing can be created or destroyed. Quantum physics takes this much further, stating that an atom is basically a vacuum with no physical structure. It is made of invisible energy, not tangible material, just the way that religious and spiritual teachers describe spirit.

There is another exciting theory known as biocentrism that has been put forward by Professor Robert Lanza, an expert in regenerative medicine and Adjunct Professor at Wake Forest University School of Medicine. This theory states that consciousness is at the centre of the very fabric of the universe. Scientists had always believed that physical matter came first but Lanza proffers that consciousness creates the material universe.

Lanza's theory implies that death of consciousness is impossible and only exists as a

147

thought because people identify themselves with their bodies. Most people believe that, because their body will someday die, then their consciousness will also perish. If the body generates consciousness then consciousness dies with the body but if the body receives consciousness in the same way that a satellite box receives signals, then consciousness continues, even when the physical body dies. Lanza's theory of quantum consciousness offers a scientific explanation for phenomenon such as near-death experiences and past lives.

After all this research on religion, spirituality and scientific theories on life and death, I pause to consider if I now have a better understanding of my connection with Sue. I certainly feel I have moved from asking questions about my own experiences and those of my family to encompass a much larger picture that involves the entire universe and the meaning of life. Quite a tall order, I must admit! It does seem though that we are each here for a specific reason, to complete a personal mission, to gain a particular experience or to develop a certain trait. There are many beliefs and theories to back-up the view that we have lived before in other eras and that we usually reincarnate in soul groups, sometimes within the same family.

Ultimately, everything points to our need to grow in awareness, to become more light-filled, which means developing compassion, respect and empathy for all other lifeforms. Living an authentic life, despite the many influences and constraints that demand conformity, are also important traits to develop. The intent of all forms of spirituality is to reduce the effects of ego that cause divisions and alienate others, to honour every person's freewill and to respect all beings. All religions and spiritual teachings tell us that we are each part of God-consciousness, that ultimately we are all one. Even science is moving towards the concept that consciousness is at the heart of life and is ever-lasting.

I know there is still the question of how all of this has fitted in with my understanding of Sue's early demise in 1932 and her spirit's asserted reincarnation into a new life as her niece in Wexford Town in 1964. The concept that souls often incarnate in soul groups certainly explains why it may have been that our spirit (Sue's and mine) passed through the same family unit. Then there was the reason for Sue's unfulfilled life and early exit from an earth life. Brendan had said in the first reading that Sue hadn't achieved certain experiences that her soul had required to advance spiritually and that, in this life, I had actually experienced these events. This was the reason, according to Brendan, that our soul had to come back and try again, to fulfil whatever plan or learn whatever lesson we have chosen to master at a spirit level.

Reincarnation makes perfect sense to me at an intellectual level. It is only at an emotional level, rooted as I am in a physical body, that it all sounds incredible. Then again, the whole cycle of life and death is pretty mystifying, with or without reincarnation. From all the philosophies and religious teachings I have come across on this journey of exploration, reincarnation seems the most likely explanation for creation to me. It is certainly the fairest, as souls get a second chance, and a third chance, and this goes on infinitum, until awareness finally dawns.

When it comes to the final question of whether or not I feel I am the reincarnation of Sue, I am definitely tending to veer towards the 'Yes' side of the spectrum. There are just so many personal experiences, readings from strangers that knew nothing about me, coincidences that I can't explain and the regression that took me back to see through the eyes of Sue at various times in her life. I have noted down a number of these in the following table that are particularly compelling. I do feel I am on an eternal journey, that I have lived before and will very likely live again in another body, until I reunite with my soul group, this time for keeps.

Links Discovered Between Lucy Costigan and Sue Costigan

Lucy Costigan	Sue Costigan	Source
I have been fascinated by glass decanters and crystal since childhood	Sue worked in the Portmarnock Golf Club as waitress and bar assistant, surrounded by the finest decanters and finely cut glass	My experience
I loved the sound and movement of the Charleston from the first time I heard it, at age 11	Sue learned to dance the Charleston during the hectic '20s and loved it	My experience/ Information passed on by my family
I loved the fashion of the '20s and actively sought out the look in my early 20s	Sue lived during the 1920s and hence this is the fashion style she wore	My experience
I had recurring dreams and thoughts of a man with a bouquet of white roses, when I had no knowledge of the significance of this	Tom put a bouquet of white roses on Sue's grave	My experience/ Information passed on by my family
I was told that I had lived a life in the 1920s, not reaching my 30s, and that family from that incarnation were still with me.	Sue had died in 1932, aged 20. Three of her siblings were part of my life at that time, including her brother, Mike, my father.	Spiritual Reading with Brendan O'Callaghan, March 27 1990/Facts
I was told a sea-faring man from the same time as Sue wanted to make contact with me.	My great-grand father, Michael Flynn was a ship's carpenter during the late 1800s, early 1900s, and was alive during part of Sue's life.	Spiritual Reading with Brendan O'Callaghan, March 27 1990/ Facts

Lucy Costigan	Sue Costigan	Source
I was told there was room made for me to live my current life, as though I had to be squeezed in, and that I was born unexpectedly.	My mother never expected to be able to give birth, after having two miscarriages and a still birth. She had to stay in bed under doctor's care for six months before I was born. I was most unexpected.	Spiritual Reading with Brendan O'Callaghan, March 27 1990/ Information passed on by my family
I became vegetarian from around the age of 7 and, as a child, I had a fear of blood.	Sue was coaxed to drink animal's blood to boost her poor condition during her illness.	My experience/ Information passed on by my family.
I exhibited a fear of riding on a motorbike.	Sue had ridden from Wexford to Rosslare Harbour on the back of Tom's motorbike and it is presumed that is how she caught cold, leading to the onset of TB and to her early death.	My experience/ Information passed on by my family.
I was told that my previous life was in Edwardian times (1901 to 1910) and that I had been constricted then, finding it hard to breathe.	Sue was born in 1911 and had been constricted by the onset of TB, but also in her early upbringing that hindered her self-expression.	Angel Reading with Linda Shalloe, May 2014/Facts and My interpretation of family dynamics
I was told that Sue and I were soul twins and that Sue had suffered from chest complaints.	Sue suffered from chest complaints during the onset of TB.	Spiritual Reading with Maura, February 2019/Facts.

IN SEARCH OF TOM

I often wondered what had become of Sue's love, Tom. There was little information to go on. I wondered if he'd married and if he'd lived a long life. I hoped he'd found happiness after the depth of sadness and loss he'd endured as a young man, after Sue's death.

Since the regression evening in May 2015, I had largely put Sue's story behind me, only referring to it occasionally, with family or close friends. There was one event though that brought it back when I went for a final reading with Maura in Kilkenny for my birthday in February 2019. She asked that I bring two photos, so I brought my two favourites, the one of Sue, Tom and Cha taken in Portmarnock, circa 1928, and also one of my parents, taken around the time they got engaged.

Maura took up the Portmarnock photo first. She pointed to Sue and asked straight away if anyone had ever told me that I was this girl in a past life. I said yes, I had been told that.

Maura closed her eyes and took a deep breath. Then she said, "I feel she suffered from chest complaints."

I affirmed that this was correct.

"She is a twin of yours, like a soul twin; you are very close," she said.

153

Then turning her attention to Cha on the right she closed her eyes again. "Cancer. She knew her body was on its way out. There's an England connection, Birmingham or Blackpool..."

"She honeymooned in Brighton," I corrected.

Maura continued. "I'm going along a path and the grave is to the right. You will be going there, back to Dublin."

I was impressed at Maura's interpretation of events under spirit guidance. I loved the explanation of 'soul twin' she had given for Sue and me. Later, I looked for an explanation of this term as I'd never heard the expression before. There are several interpretations but the essence is that one soul becomes so advanced that it needs to split in two. The twin souls then continue on their earth missions, with the soul becoming manifest through two separate lives. Soul twins are different than soulmates: whereas soulmates are two different souls that share a spiritual bond over many lifetimes, twin souls are basically two halves of the same soul. Interesting!

Next she turned her attention to my parent's engagement photo.

"They are a very handsome couple," Maura smiled down at their portraits. "Your Dad is proud of you," she said. "He's telling me you've come through a lot of tough times but he's proud you've done well." Then Maura smiled. "He's saying he didn't believe in any of this when he was here but now he's thanking me for giving him this facility."

"Your mother is here too," she said. "She's saying in a jokey way that one of them married beneath themselves but that none of that matters now."

I was stunned at this. I knew what it referred to. When my dad began going seriously with my mam, his mother and sister, May, were supposedly raging because he had never had a steady girlfriend and they presumed he would always be there to look after them. Also, mammy was a noted beauty and an accomplished dancer and singer. There was a lot of jealousy and bad-mouthing that had no substance, only caused by their fear of being left alone in the house, without Dad's support. Despite his relatives' misgivings, Mike and Kathleen were married on March 26 1951. They rented a house in St. Mary's Terrace in Rosslare Harbour for eleven years, before settling in Wexford Town.

It was a case of old family squabbles being aired and then allowed to evaporate. It was good to hear that in the spirit world all this could be joked about, seen in the context of a distant event on earth, when souls were still learning lessons and certain skills needed to be fine-tuned.

On the day of the reading, Maura also told me something that caused me much anxiety. She said that two family members would be going back to spirit within a short space of time. When I questioned her, she said she wasn't told who these people were but that it would be devastating for me. This was really hard to hear and I really wished I hadn't gone to her. I tried to put it behind me and to get on with day to day living.

I really thought that was the end of all of it, the readings and the exploration of my connection with

Sue. It was an unexpected phone-call from Brendan in July 2019 that ignited my quest once again. Just talking to Brendan transported me back to the 1990s and the early days of the Spiritual Centre, when spirit seemed more real than anything in the tangible world. Brendan knew about the book I had written in 2010 with my nephew, Michael Cullen, called *Strangest Genius*, about the Irish stained-glass artist, Harry Clarke. I mentioned that we had just finished the sequel, *Dark Beauty* that was going to be published in October, 2019.

"The 1920s really hold something special for me," I said.

Brendan laughed. 'You feel at home there'.

That was so true! In 2012 I had written a biography of Arthur Kingsley Porter, a Harvard professor of archaeology and multi-millionaire who disappeared off the coast of Donegal. It should have been obvious, but I seriously hadn't put two and two together until I was chatting with Brendan. Both Harry Clarke (1889-1931) and Kingsley Porter (1883-1933) had lived in Dublin during the height of the 1920s. Clarke was from North Frederick Street, while Kingsley Porter and his wife, Lucy, had stayed in the Shelbourne Hotel on various occasions during the 1920s. I loved researching this period. There was a buzz and an excitement that drew me in every time.

The book launch for *Strangest Genius* was held in May 2010 in Bewley's Café, an iconic establishment on Grafton Street, Dublin, since 1927. Harry Clarke's six decorative windows, dating back to 1927 and 1928, really sparkled that evening. Then in November 2012, my book, *Glenveagh Mystery*, was launched in the exquisite Glenveagh Castle, in Co. Donegal. Porter's library, decorated when he and his wife first arrived in the castle in 1929, remains practically unaltered since that time. This had all been Sue's era and I couldn't help feeling that her energy had always been gently steering me back into the styles, the settings and the period in which she had lived.

Brendan and I said we'd keep in contact and we ended the call. That evening, something had been stirred by our conversation and I felt uneasy. My thoughts returned to Tom and I felt there was something still to be done before I could let it all slip into the past. Within the week, I felt compelled to begin the search for Tom. Ultimately, I knew I needed to write our story: Sue's and mine.

I enlisted the help of my sister, Theresa, who has the uncanny ability to zoom in on tiny details that ultimately prove to be so vital to the unfolding of the whole picture. We had scant information to go on. We knew Tom's surname, but we didn't know the name of his parents, his age, his date of birth or date of death. The only snippet we had was Dad's remembrance of Tom's address all those years ago—a particular house number on a road in Sutton, Co. Dublin. Of course, having so many records freely available and digitised, such as the 1901 and 1911 Census, and the Irish Genealogy website, we could explore so many documents from the late 1800s and early 1900s from the comfort of our armchairs.

My first task was to locate where Tom was buried. I remembered my walk with Philo thirty years earlier when we had visited St. Mary's

Cemetery in Howth and he had promised someday to take me to St. Fintan's Cemetery in Sutton. So while I combed the internment records of these cemeteries in the Fingal area, where I presumed Tom's remains would have been buried, Theresa navigated the online census of 1911 and the Irish genealogical website, where church and state certificates can be freely accessed.

It took us several weeks to finally put all of the pieces together. We began by finding Tom's burial record. We subsequently found that his age had been incorrectly inscribed on the internment record, through discovering several family members, including a sister, who were also interred in the same grave. Dad's memory had been incredibly accurate as the house number he had given was correct and the road he had remembered just needed a slight adjustment before we found a match. Then we progressed to the Census and finally found a family of eight children that included Tom and his sister of the ages we were seeking. This led to finding Tom's birth record on the newly digitised Irish genealogical site. From other websites, we gathered details of his family, finally arriving at the main details of Tom's life.

I was ecstatic to have finally found him and to know that he had lived a full life, marrying in the 1940s and going on to have seven children. He had lived his whole life in the Sutton area. He was born in March 1907, making him over four years older than Sue. It was also fascinating to see that, like Sue, his father had been a train driver, having worked his way up from fireman, so it's no wonder he was welcomed into Sue's family so readily. Both families also took in lodgers.

I wondered then, if Tom had ever spoken to his wife or family about Sue, and the loss he had suffered all those years before. There was always the chance that he had kept Sue's letters, but it was only a slim one. Sue's family must have destroyed all of Tom's letters, probably because they were very personal or reminded them of their grief. There was no way that I would encroach on Tom's family but I just mused that possibly somewhere Sue's letters might exist.

Tom had died in early 1982, at the age of 74. I would have been 18 then and beginning to have thoughts and dreams about a man who had lovingly put flowers on Sue's grave. I was shocked to find that Tom's remains were interred in St. Fintan's Cemetery, Sutton. This was the cemetery that Philo had promised to take me to, all those years before, in 1989. Life seemed to be coming full-circle.

18. Michael Cullen and I at book signing of 'Strangest Genius'

19. Portmarnock Golf Club, 2019

20. Corridor of Portmarnock Golf Club, 2019

21. Trophies and awards, Portmarnock Golf Club, 2019

PORTMARNOCK GOLF CLUB, 2019

After this journey of exploration and discoveries across decades and centuries, there was still one place I had to visit, Pormarnock Golf Club, the scene of so much joy and the awakening of love for Sue, during the late 1920s.

The Club has come a long way since it was first established by William Chalmers Pickeman and George Ross in December 1894. The 18-hole golf links is constantly ranked among the top golf courses in the world and it has been graced by some of the finest players in the game, such as Arnold Palmer, Tiger Woods, Padraig Harrington and Rory McIlroy. Its setting, on the edge of a long, narrow peninsula, is quite spectacular.

In the summer of 1990, just a few months after my initial reading with Brendan, I was invited to the afters of a wedding in Portmarnock. I was full of excitement leading up to the evening, being convinced that I would surely feel something for the place, after finding out that Sue had worked there. This was before the days of the Internet, when you didn't have the luxury of looking-up anything that took your fancy. I went to the wedding with a group of workmates and, although the hotel was magnificent, I was duly disappointed that I felt nothing, no vibes, no memories, nothing. It was only later that I discovered that this was the Portmarnock Hotel and Golf Links, whose present building had been constructed upon the original family home of the Jameson family. It had nothing whatsoever to do with the Portmarnock Golf Club that was located three kilometres south on the peninsula.

Finally, in the winter of 1997, I visited the club. I travelled by bus to Portmarnock Village with my cousin, Raymond. Then we walked along the peninsula where we had lovely views of the sea. I had never seen a photo of the club house and I thought it was a very elegant building, painted white with a red roof. We entered the small reception area and it was deserted, perhaps because it was wintertime and off-season. We walked down the wood-panelled corridor, peered into the presentation cases that displayed various golf trophies and perused the photos and boards on the walls, where captains' names were engraved that dated back to the last century. I hoped to find a photograph of the Carrs but there was none displayed, except one of Joe Carr in his early years. I wondered if the Club had any photos of the staff dating from the 1920s.

I don't know what I was really expecting that day. The only feeling I had was that I was walking on hallowed ground. Looking back, I must have been overwhelmed by it all. It was too difficult to take in the enormity of the whole past-life assertion. It was certainly fascinating and made for endless speculation but it made me feel freakish. I mean, no one ever talked about past lives, unless it was mentioned as a joke, that the guy down the pub had told the lads he was Napoleon, or a rather eccentric woman dreamed of living in Ancient Egypt as Cleopatra. Throughout my life, the shadow of the 1920s had played out around me and I had often thought of Sue, but she had been part of my family and it simply may have been the tragedy of it all that somehow filtered into my psyche. That was a much simpler proposition than accepting that I had lived a lifetime in another body, in another time.

Raymond and I spent just a short time that day in Portmarnock, not even venturing into the other rooms, as there was still no one around. Then we boarded the bus back into the city. I always planned to return someday on a proper visit, when there would be plenty of time for sitting down to tea in the dining room and really soaking up the atmosphere.

In the intervening years I had emailed the club, enquiring if there were any records of staff, naming my relatives, the Carrs, who had worked there in the 1920s and '30s. I was particularly hoping to find a photo of the Carrs because I couldn't find one anywhere. I was disappointed not to receive a reply. I did, however, discover in T. M Healy's centenary book on the club that all staff records were burned in the fire of 1950.

On September 12, 2019, the scene was set to revisit Portmarnock. It had been over twenty years since my previous short excursion. I travelled with my partner, Tony, my sister, Theresa and my nephew, Michael. Our first call of the day was to St. MacCullin's Church in Lusk, where we were filming the Harry Clarke windows there as part of the documentary we were making, entitled, *Journey through glass.* Once filming was out of the way, we drove south towards Portmarnock.

We took a right at the village and turned on to the peninsula. About half way down, our path was blocked by a gate. Michael pressed the buzzer, spoke to the receptionist and we were summarily admitted. The Club House looked radiant, like a sprawling country mansion, still white and red-roofed, overlooking the sea, with fine views towards Sutton and all along the bay. The smell of the sea was intoxicating. A few gents were teeing off as we arrived. This time, there was a friendly man at reception. We passed down the long corridor that was now displaying even more trophies, glass tables and memorabilia than the last time I had been there.

We took a seat in a small dining room and were given menus by a young girl, dressed in a black uniform and white blouse. I couldn't sit down though. I walked around with Michael, pouring over the photos on the walls, and even managing to get a glimpse of the bar upstairs. I was sure this was new. Instinctively, I knew that this was where the staff quarters had been located, upstairs and out of sight.

My feelings and senses were on high alert that afternoon, completely different from that first short visit I'd made all those years ago with Raymond. It was as though the floodgates had finally opened and I was actually tapping into something real inside myself that held a key to Sue's old life. I needed so badly to get outside, to breathe in the sea air and to gaze across the bay. This is what Sue and Tom had done so often, I just knew it. There had always been stuffiness inside, an attitude of superiority. At times, this must have been stifling, with layers of elitism being celebrated by male-only membership and wealthy, powerful clientele. May, being the eldest of the girls and the first to be employed, must have felt a responsibility to keep her sisters behaving in an exemplary manner, when serving 'their betters' or doing basic chores. May had always been a surrogate mother to her siblings. She also revelled in the position she held in Portmarnock and took great pride in it. It was sad and indeed outrageous that in many ways May had seen herself as being socially beneath the men she served. This was the society she had lived in, where there was little opportunity to challenge the traditions and the warped values of the time.

I had no doubt now that it was Sue and Cha who had laughed late into the night. Only two years had separated them and I was certain that they had been very close. I could clearly imagine Sue and Tom taking too many breaks outside, chatting and laughing, as though they didn't have a care in the world. As a child, May had often called me a 'giddy gooly' whenever I got a fit of laughter. I wondered if she had had a similar name for Sue. Anyway, I'm sure it was all that May could do to keep tabs on that skitterish threesome.

Back in this life, Michael took photos while I walked along the pathways, lost in thought. Then it was back inside to the dining room. A manager asked politely if we were guests of any members. "We're visitors," Tony answered. We were lucky we were allowed to remain. Afterwards, we all laughed that we could have said, "Do you want the long story or the short one." I don't think the staff members would have been impressed though if we had revealed our true reason for being there. It was still afternoon and none of the golfers had come in to dine yet, although the large dining room to our right was being set for dinner. We were relieved that we had the small room to ourselves while we ate a light meal.

When we finished, Michael was out of his chair, taking more photographs and exploring. Theresa was sitting to the right of Tony while I was sitting to his left. "It reminds me of the photo," Theresa said. "There were two sisters at either side of Tom and now there are two sisters at either side of Tony!"

I had to smile. The old threesome that had shared so many adventures together in this very building were now being remembered and honoured by another threesome: two Costigan sisters and my partner, Tony, who just happened to have the same surname as Sue's boyfriend: Walsh. Tony's family had originally spelt their name with an 'e', the exact same spelling as Tom's surname. It was indeed surreal.

I was happy when we were back in the car and heading home. The four of us were glad we had been admitted to the club and had managed to be served. None of us had felt comfortable though. I felt full of half-memories and surfacing emotions. Without Tom, Cha and May it was only a pretty view and an historical building. I knew for sure then that there was nothing left for me in Portmarnock.

That evening, I was filled with thoughts of Tom and Sue, all that they had felt for each other and the fun they'd had. For some reason, I thought of Philo then, of how I had been so attracted to him the first time we'd met at work, the suit he'd been wearing that had offset his dark hair to perfection. Looking back now, he had a definite look of Tom in that faded Portmarnock photo. Tom was over four years older than Sue. Philo was five years older than me. Both had lived in the Sutton area. There was one major difference though. I had never won Philo's heart, though I was certain that Sue had been Tom's sweetheart.

In the following days, I thought a lot about my family over the last four generations. It was a lovely autumn day when I took the short trip to Rosslare Harbour with Tony and Theresa. Walking along the little strand that still remains there, I was struck by the peace I felt, despite the work of the port, the ships and the terminal that surrounded us. This was a haven for Sue and her siblings as children; for my parents and my siblings when they lived here; for Ray and the McGoverns when they visited, as they frequently did as children. I was reminded of each of them as I walked along the seashore and the influence they have each had on my life.

Since I was catapulted on this journey in March, 1990, to unearth all I could about my connection with Sue, I have also discovered family secrets, negative patterns and old wounds that I have no doubt influence my family and myself today. That day, walking along the strand in the Harbour, I felt the need for some kind of healing at a family level to really let go of the past. It wasn't long before the next step of the journey was presented to me.

170

ANCESTRAL HEALING

I met my good friend, Isabel, in town for our usual coffee and chat. She told me about the work of Fr. Jim Cogley, parish priest in Our Lady's Island in Co. Wexford, psychotherapist, wood carver and author who specialises in ancestral healing. I was immediately drawn to the concept. That evening, I checked the net and found that Jim was conducting a series of workshops on this very topic the following month. I enrolled along with Tony, Theresa and Isabel for two full-day sessions and I also sent for Jim's book on the subject.

While waiting to attend the workshops, I came across an article by Maria Moran, a psychotherapist with a particular interest in ancestral healing. It stated that we often live-out family scripts that are embedded in us at an unconscious level, that greatly influence us. These scripts may be positive, such as leaving us a wise legacy of how to live a happy life, but they can also distort our thinking and lead to negative life-choices. According to Maria, "the core issue may go back several generations...resulting in the same dynamic being set up time and time again and so we discover that the same misfortunes that our forebears endured are found to repeat themselves in future generations."

Just like a physical trait or a genetic bias, beliefs, values and personality traits can be passed down in families over centuries. Ancestral healing recognises these family scripts that are a source of dysfunctional patterns of behaviour. This can lead to a new awareness, as part of a healing process that frees us up to make new, better choices.

In the Costigan family, I already knew some of the positive traits that had been passed down, such as a strong work ethic and the nurturing of close family ties. I wondered if undertaking study in this area would give me greater insights into negative or destructive patterns that have filtered down, carried by my ancestors through generations.

The result of attending the workshops was to gain further insights into the branches of my direct family line and also to appraise my family in a wider social context. There were some pointers that participants on the workshop were given, such as to look out for family members who were missing from the family tree or any recurring issues that seemed to plague a branch of the family. We were advised to research our family trees if this was possible, but more importantly, to use our intuition to unearth negative patterns that still impinge on our families and ourselves today.

There was little doubt that anyone living in Ireland in the early 1900s had major political conflicts to grapple with, on both a national and a global level. There were religious, cultural and social traditions that had to be respected in an age when freedom of conscience and choice of lifestyle were mere aspirations. It was also an age when gender roles were clearly defined. I was most interested to unearth predominant traits in my family that had prevailed through the centuries, influencing and perhaps stifling the present generation. I wanted to get some sense of the values that my ancestors had lived by.

I began by unearthing the Flynn side of my family roots. Michael Flynn Senior, my great-great grandfather, was a surveyor and a civil engineer in Cork. His son, also Michael Flynn Junior–the seafarer referred to in Brendan's reading–was a shipwright, also a well-paid and respected position at the time. In the 1800s, a lot of trades were declining in Cork, but shipbuilding was thriving as Cork Harbour was a major port for trans-Atlantic trade. Michael Junior married Charlotte Lucy Johnson, a publican whose parents had emigrated from Scotland. At a time when so many families found their breadwinner to be unemployed, the Flynn's public house in Glanmire Road, coupled with Michael's income as a shipwright, insured a steady income, putting the family in good social standing. Their eldest daughter, Margaret Lucy, married my grandfather, Nicholas Costigan, a train driver, a highly sought-after occupation with a stable income.

While I was researching the Flynn family branch, I had some interesting correspondence from Raymond. He had found out from another relative that my grandmother had inherited £155 pounds from her mother's estate in 1904, just before she married Pop. I found a website that estimated that £150 in 1900 would be equivalent to around €17,500 in 2017, a sizeable nest-egg for any recently married couple.

I always had the sense that my grandmother had felt a cut above the rest, being middle-class and living in a large house in Rosslare Harbour. She was definitely comfortable and wanted for little, at a time of great social and political upheaval. From her bedroom window, she had a good vantage point, where she humorously labelled her neighbours, many of whom she felt socially superior to. Her children were reared in this environment, where they were expected to behave with exemplary manners and to attain either a satisfactory career or a suitable husband. There were certainly a lot of social and moral pressures placed on the girls to act with decorum and to live up to their social standing. Positions for the three Costigan daughters in Portmarnock Golf Club would have been looked on very favourably.

There was also Cha's union with the studious and steady Charles McGovern to consider. This would have been seen as an advantageous marriage, as Charles was a CIE clerk who had already passed several exams that had earned him rapid promotion. I know my dad had always enjoyed long conversations with Charlie, as they were both very well-read and knowledgeable on many subjects. Sadly, it requires a good deal of intimacy before the inner nature of a person becomes visible, whether light-filled and benevolent or dark, damaged and menacing. Family pressures played a significant role in bringing my aunt Cha and Charlie together. The resulting marriage and subsequent troubled home brought much heartache and division that has continued into the present generation.

It appears that in the early 1900s, a streak of superiority and high-expectations was set in motion. Failure by children to live up to parental expectations led to feelings of inferiority and powerlessness. Over the past century, this has resulted in excessive self-criticism, negativity, a crippling lack of personal power, and fear of expression of feelings and opinions that has caused deep frustration and stunted individual fulfilment among some family members. Being overly concerned by what others think—by the values that they live by while not paying enough heed to one's own moral compass—is a recipe for disaster.

Then there were the secrets I uncovered. In the Costigan line, there was a member of our family who was ostracised to such an extent that his own nieces and nephews never knew of his existence. The true facts only came to light when Raymond found the birth certificate of James Costigan, brother of Pop and uncle to Sue and her siblings, who my dad and his siblings had never heard of.

The Census of 1911 threw further light on the facts. Just a year after Pop's marriage, James married a widow, Hannah, who had two children from a previous marriage. Whether it was for this, or for some other reason that James was cut-off from his family of origin without trace, remains unknown. He worked as a foundry labourer and lived in Bow Street, in the heart of Dublin. James died in the old South Dublin Union Workhouse in 1920, from heart failure, at the aged of 49. His wife, Hannah, had died before him. Almost one hundred years later, it is sad to hear that my grand-uncle, James, died without his only brother, Pop, ever knowing about his whereabouts. There was no further light ever shed on Pop's disowned brother but it seems to speak of an abandonment that occurred because of some family value that wasn't adhered to.

In my spiritual reading with Linda, she picked up that Sue's self-expression had been stifled. There's no doubt that Sue's life really opened up when she got to Dublin and met Tom. These were very freeing years for Sue when she danced, rode on the back of a motorbike and began to break old patterns, developing a new confidence. In my second reading with Brendan, my grandmother was supposedly working with our family to help empower its members. Perhaps this was her way of addressing some of the restrictive values she had unwittingly helped to cement during her lifetime, such as an over-reliance on social mores and cultural dictates, and a stifling of self-belief, openness and self-expression.

Being of equal value to all, no matter what you choose to do in life or your financial standing, is a new paradigm that this generation needs to embrace on the road to healing old patterns. The way forward is to acknowledge the mistakes of the past, to understand the fears and limiting beliefs that caused so much heartache. It is time to forgive all involved for propagating these confining values and to move on, a great deal wiser.

The biggest revelation of all, though, was discovering that Pop had suffered so many devastating losses. He was the second youngest of seven, yet his own children believed that he only had two sisters, Mary Anne, the eldest girl, and Susanna Frances. Four of his siblings were written out of our family history. I wondered why this had happened. I already knew about James, Pop's elder brother, as outlined above. It was only by trawling through digitised civil records that I discovered the existence of Pop's sister, Kate (1864-1874), called after her mother, who tragically died at ten years old. Then I located another two siblings, Bridget (1870-1872) and Pop's younger brother, William (1874-1877), who had both sadly died at two years of age. The losses that Pop had suffered began to drastically mount up. Then there was his sister, Susanna, who had married Thomas Sheridan, a clerk, who lived in James St. They had one son, John. I had never known until I searched through family records that Susanna had died at the age of 41 on 27 September 1911, just days before my grandparents' third daughter was born. Susanna Frances, known as Sue, was named after her recently deceased aunt.

Pop had learned to stoically bottle-up all his grief, just like so many did in those days. He had tried to get on with his family life and his work as best he could. It is no wonder that the death of his youngest daughter, Susanna, at the age of 20, finally almost unhinged him. It may have been a long established pattern, whereby those who died tragically in the family were white-washed out of our history, in a mistaken belief that, in so doing, grief would be lessened. In reality of course, grief unexpressed remains unhealed, leading to a deadening of emotion. My own father had also followed suit, never openly talking about his sister

Sue's death or the miscarriages and stillbirth that he and my mam had endured in silence together, and the inevitable pain that lay buried.

Releasing traits of ignorance, powerlessness, abuse, poverty, addictions and patterns of secrecy that stifle expression, ultimately becomes a way of freeing present and future generations from being enslaved by the negative bonds of the past. I know it is not my direct line, but my aunt Cha and subsequent generations have suffered due to skewered values around money that were passed down from her husband, Charlie. In one of the workshops I did with Jim Cogley, he talked about poverty consciousness and how it can pass down and ruin families over generations. The fear of not having enough and always needing to accumulate more may have its origins in some deep trauma, maybe centuries ago, such as a family eviction or some gross injustice. We may never know the true source of the intense emotions and destructive behaviours that have been passed down but the negative energy that lives on today may be all too real.

Some of our most negative patterns of behaviour are so engrained, creating tangles and knots through countless generations, that we may well wonder if they can ever be undone. The first step I have learned is to at least acknowledge that a pattern exists that is causing some family members great suffering. Maybe then we may find a way to begin to untangle the mess left behind by our ancestors. If there is a way of stopping the pain and destruction from continuing, then all the work will have been well worth it. Maybe then it will be possible to change the negative scripts and to embrace the gifts that are also part of our heritage.

Ancestral healing also allows for ancestral memory, where experiences or emotions may be passed down from one member of a generation to another. I had given this some thought when I had first gone for my first reading with Brendan, almost thirty years previously. I had to bear in mind that this was yet another theory as to why I had been so in tune with Sue's life and the era she grew up in. However, it didn't take account of the readings I'd had with Brendan and other clairvoyants, unless they were picking up information from my ancestors and misinterpreting them as past life experiences. Ancestral memory still seemed a poor fit for specific memories, experiences and preferences, such as those I had felt around Sue and her era. After attending the ancestral healing workshops though and gaining new understanding and insights, I felt that other layers of Sue's and my family's story could be finally consigned to the past.

LAYING IT ALL TO REST

After so much researching and soul-searching, it certainly feels that closure for Sue and I is close at hand. Closure is needed for me as I allow my own past to settle so that I can more fully focus on my life today; closure for Sue, so that her traumatic experiences of sickness, death and loss may fade into the light; closure for our family, now that we have attempted to invoke and facilitate healing for those living and for those who have long since passed to another realm.

We are all familiar with the power of ritual, to mark a celebration, a rite of passage or the passing of a loved one. I had never been drawn to visiting graves as I had always felt the spirit of the departed was living in another dimension and certainly would have no need to be hanging around a graveyard! But I did feel it was only fitting that I follow my heart and go on a journey to visit the remains of the main players in this drama: Tom in St. Fintan's, Howth; Cha in Deansgrange Cemetery, Blackrock; Dad and Mam in Crosstown, Wexford; Sue, along with her parents and sister May, her brother Joe, his wife May and baby son, in St. Ruane's, Kilrane, Rosslare Harbour. I wanted to give each a special gift, to thank them for the part they have played in my life and continue to play. It seemed obvious what I would bring to each.

The first trip was to visit Tom's remains, to thank him for his love and kindness. Of late, I had felt he was close by, gently nudging me along on this journey. I also needed to tell him he was completely exonerated, just in case he had ever felt guilty for bringing Sue home on his motorbike, when she had had her tonsils removed. Fate and the stars had not been aligned for Tom and Sue in that life and they had little choice but to try to deal with the hands that had been dealt to both of them.

On a lovely autumn day, the plan was to travel to St. Fintan's Cemetery in Sutton, after we had filmed an interview for our Harry Clarke film in Balbriggan, and to head on then to Deansgrange. Beforehand, I had called the lady responsible for cemetery records at Fingal County Council and had been given the approximate location of Tom's grave in St. Fintan's. I had also arranged to meet my cousin, Raymond, later that afternoon, at the main gates of Deansgrange.

We passed the road where Tom had lived and I actually got to see his former home. He'd had a wonderful view of the bay, a sweeping panorama all the way out to the Portmarnock Peninsula. Then it was on to St. Fintan's. The cemetery is set on a hill overlooking the sea. It didn't take long to find Tom and his family's grave. I was so delighted to finally find him. I imagined how Sue couldn't wait for that first glimpse of Tom when she'd returned to Portmarnock, after spending a few days back home. Strange and all as it seemed, this really felt like a reunion. Tony and Theresa came over beside me as I placed the bouquet of white roses in the centre. "Just returning the favour, Tom," I smiled.

Tom had known deep loss and heartache in his life with Sue's death but also in later life, as I had recently discovered. Tragedy had struck again when Tom's teenage son was involved in a fatal traffic accident when riding his motorbike. I just hoped that, wherever Tom's loving and gentle spirit resided, he was happy now and engaged in further fulfilling adventures in the spirit realm.

Then it was time to head south to Blackrock, to visit Cha's resting place, in Deansgrange Cemetery. Raymond had got there before us and had already found the grave, leaving a bunch of autumnal flowers. He initially had some reservations about visiting the grave where his father resided, the father who he remembered as being "a tyrant" and seriously neglectful of his family's basic needs. I was so pleased though he had decided to come with us. We had emailed each other the previous day, as we had done several times a week for many years. I had urged Raymond to meet us, as this visit was part of a wider circle of healing for all of our ancestors and their descendants. I still understood the conflicting emotions that Raymond was experiencing.

Raymond led us left along a path that ran beside the cemetery wall. Then we turned right, just as Maura had foretold in her reading. Just another few steps and we arrived at the grave. The remains of Charlotte, her husband, Charles, their son-in-law, Fionàn, and Charlie's aunt, Ann, are buried there. My nephew, Michael, placed the white roses in the centre. Theresa gave Raymond some holy water to sprinkle, in the hope of bringing healing to the many troubles that had dampened each of their lives while on earth. Deep divisions and rifts still existed in this branch of my family and I silently wondered if anything could bring about understanding, healing and closure.

I turned my attention to Cha and her fun-loving spirit. I had always felt Sue and Cha had been especially close. I remembered her standing with Tom and Sue in Portmarnock and I imagined those nights long ago when two sisters danced the Charleston in a Dublin dancehall, when neither had a care in the world.

The afternoon remained sunny as we chatted with Raymond about deeds of the past and concerns of the present. Then we drove to a coffee shop for refreshments, almost like a meeting between family and friends after a funeral, when loved ones are remembered and the time shared with them is cherished. Raymond was in great spirits, delighted he had at long last revisited his mother's grave. He said he understood what I was trying to do, to bring forgiveness and healing to a troubled past. We planned to meet again in November at the book launch of *Dark Beauty*, as Ray had played a significant role in the research of Harry Clarke's windows.

When we hugged before we went on our different paths, I was pleased Raymond seemed content. In the following days he was almost exuberant at having finally visited the grave, even taking a rare moment in an email to reflect on a higher power: "The spiritual power is forced on us no matter how far we try to avoid it and we forget that dimension until nothing else seems effective anymore." He also asked me if I was finally writing a book about our ancestors as we had discussed this for many years. I told him I was in the throes of writing it and planned to send him the first draft in the next few months.

Two days later found us at Mam and Dad's grave in St. Ibar's Cemetery, just a short distance across the bridge from Wexford Town. It was a rainy afternoon but there was a great sense of peace there. This time Theresa placed the roses on their grave, for all the love and guidance they had both given us throughout their lifetimes. Many happy moments that we had shared together flitted across my mind. Life is really very short, I felt, as I stood there. When all the drama has passed, all that's left is connection, all that lasts is love. It was also Theresa's birthday so that added an extra sparkle to the occasion.

The evening before I planned to visit Sue's grave, I placed the flowers I had prepared for her on the Edwardian sideboard that has a special place in my home. This has been in our family for well over a century, having been bought by my grandparents when they settled in Rosslare Harbour in 1911. The old decanters I bought as a child are still displayed there, along with a 1920s dark lady that I purchased in Roches Stores when I first moved to Dublin in 1986. Of course, the photo of Sue, Tom and Cha takes pride of place. I looked into the mirror and recalled all those before me who have gazed in at their reflections, perhaps taking a moment to pat their hair and check their appearance before venturing out into the world. Sue would have definitely stood here, before scampering off to the beach as a child or to dance in the Rosslare Harbour Social Club as a teenager.

After all those uncanny connections and intersections with the 1920s during my lifetime, the readings, the regression, ancestral healing, our aunt-niece relationship, the concept of twin souls and the enormity of one soul living two lives, I am ready to blend and mix the best of us. I embrace Sue's confidence and zest for life. I soak up her daring and adventurous spirit. For my part, I will provide the means of expressing the essence of our lives and chronicling our experiences.

The following day, I set out on the short journey to visit Sue's remains and all the family members who had witnessed her joys and sorrows. After stopping to lay flowers on my uncle Joe and his wife May's grave, we walked the short distance towards the grave that contains Sue's remains, those of her sister, May, my grandparents, and my baby cousin. After my long journey with Sue—lasting more than a century—I am glad to lay my quest to rest. I place my last bouquet of white roses for Sue, on her birthday.

EPILOGUE

On Friday, the fourth of October, 2019, when I visited Sue's grave, I really thought my book had its ending. I had been writing feverishly from August, taking just under two months to write the account of the many twists and turns of unearthing the true story about my connection with Sue. Throughout that day I got three emails from Raymond, telling me that his brother, Fintan, who had been ill for several years, was close to death. I returned Ray's last email before midnight, delighted to hear that Fintan had improved and urging Ray to rest after his long day's exertion at the hospital.

The true enormity and poignancy of the unfolding events were only made known to me later the following week when my cousin, Geraldine McGovern, Fintan's daughter, phoned from Dublin. I had been waiting for Raymond's emails all week but none had arrived. His phone had been sadly out of order so contact from that source wasn't possible. Geraldine asked me to sit down. In the week that had elapsed, Raymond and Fintan had both passed from this world, Raymond from sudden heart failure and Fintan from the ravages of his long battle with Parkinson's. Our families were shocked and devastated. Two brothers had departed within days

186

of each other. The prediction of Maura the previous February in her reading had been chilling indeed and now it had come to pass.

And so we gathered again at a graveside. This time it was Mulhuddart Cemetery, on October 16, after a requiem funeral mass that was held in Blanchardstown Church. Surrounded by family members and friends from Rosslare Harbour, Wexford and Dublin, the two brothers were laid to rest. As I stood there, this time with a single red rose to place in the open grave, I silently wondered if undertaking this journey in the months before our double-bereavement had been to spiritually prepare me, my family and perhaps most of all, Raymond, for all that was to come afterwards. I imagined both brothers being welcomed home by their many relatives in spirit, just like the scene at the end of the Titanic movie.

So many memories of Raymond and our experiences poured over me: walking along the canal on a summer's evening; watching the 1974 world cup final in our sitting room in Wexford; browsing records in the National Library; pouring over Sue's photos and scant possessions in Inchicore; editing articles for *Wexford Life*; having a marvellous meal and chat at Sharon's wedding; preparing for our interviews for RTE's *Nationwide*, filming the previous month for our new Harry Clarke film. Raymond had been such a major part of my life.

This had been a particularly difficult year for my family as in May illness had struck at the heart of our inner circle. Now we also had two significant losses to contend with. Healing from the spirit realm was never more called for as we approached the depths of winter.

The book launch of *Dark Beauty* was held on Sunday, November 17 as part of the Dublin Book Festival but it was not the same without Raymond. We dedicated our launch to his memory. I was delighted that Fintan's wife, Patricia, and my cousins, Geraldine and Julian, were there to share the afternoon with Michael, Theresa, Tony and I. I was also particularly pleased to reconnect with my cousin, Niall, after so many years. He confirmed that Sue and Cha had had a special connection. It was also lovely to hear that he had been particularly close to Cha and had enjoyed having long conversations with her. It reminded me that family ties may break us when we are subjected to the whims and ignorance of dark and troubled members. But family connections may also be a salve if, in adulthood, we choose those members to befriend who are benevolent and loving, with a wisp of wisdom to share.

In mid-December, 2019, we had another family gathering. It was the launch of our play, *The Last Day of Harry Clarke,* written by Anthony, Theresa and I. Tony had been our editor; Sharon and her husband, Martin, had been consultants on text and cover. Michael had been our book designer and technical guru. It was a lovely evening as we were also joined by Kathleen and Antoinette Costigan and by close friends. That evening, surrounded by my family, I felt really privileged to be part of such an inspiring group who are always bursting with new ideas for projects and creative pursuits.

22. Theresa, Anthony and I at book signing of 'The Last Day of Harry Clarke', 2019

After being immersed in my family's history for so many decades, I received a very apt gift for Christmas from Tony: a DNA kit so that I could take a test that would be analysed in the States, to ultimately discover my ancestry from the wider global genetic pool. It was an intriguing prospect and I couldn't wait to find out my genetic heritage. The results were fascinating: 89.5% Irish and 10.5% Viking, the latter being from my mother's ancestry. This put everything in context for me: my links with so many generations that I will never know anything about but that have greatly influenced by life.

On December 31st, 2019, as we embraced a new decade: the 2020s, I made a wish that the mistakes of the past would not be repeated. I also asked that each family member would be surrounded by healing from the highest level of light. I wasn't to know then that 2020 would be a dark year for many, as the Corona Virus brought us all into lockdown during the global pandemic.

The fear of catching the virus, with its deadly respiratory illness, was reminiscent of the worst ravages of TB that was the great scourge of the nineteenth and twentieth centuries in Europe. With every illness and death that was recorded from the Corona virus, I was once again reminded of all that Sue and her family had to endure as her illness took hold, almost ninety years previously. My heart goes out to all those who have lost loved ones to the virus. For the rest of us who are still in this world, we must continue upon our own unique journey, until the time comes to return to the fold.

REFERENCES

Buckley, D. (2010) 'The silent terror that consumed so many', The Irish Examiner, August 24, 2010.

Cockell, J. (1993), *Yesterday's Children: The Extraordinary Search for Mt Past Life Family,* London: Piatkus.

Cogley, J. (2014), *The Ancestral Self,* Wood You Believe, Volume 3, AuthorHouseUK.

Fitzgerald, F. S. [1925], *The Great Gatsby.*

Gibran, K. [1923], *The Prophet.*

Gilleece, D. (2002), *Breaking 80: The Life and Times of Joe Carr,* Dublin: Poolbeg Press,

Healy, T. M. (1993), *Portmarnock Golf Club 1894-1994: A Centenary History,* Dublin: Pormarnock Golf Club.

Jung, C. G. [1969], 'Archetypes and the Collective Unconscious' (The Collected works of C.G. Jung Vol 1, Pt 1), New Jersey: Princeton University Press.

Lanza, R. (2009), *Biocentrism: How Life and Consciousness Are the Keys to Understanding the Nature of the Universe.*

Lewis of Granada [1555], *The Sinner's Guide.*

Moran, M., *Ancestral Perspectives of the Healing Journey,* in Inside Out, Issue 58, Summer, 2009.

McMahon, P. (2015), *The Grand Design: Reflections of a Soul/Oversoul,* Volumes 1 to 6, CreateSpace.

191

McMahon, P. (2010), *There are No Goodbyes: Guided by Angels-My Tour of the Spirit World,* London: Collins.

_____*Working on the Railway in Dublin*, 1900-1925, Transcript of a talk given by Mary Muldowney in Cabra Library on 25 August 2016, accessed on 04/10/2019, https://www.dublincity.ie/story/working-railway-dublin-1900-1925-transcript

_____*UK Inflation Rate, £150 in 1900 to 2017,* http://www.in2013dollars.com/1900-GBP-in-2017?amount=150

Tapes

Spiritual Readings: March 27, 1990 and July 28, 1993, recorded on two tapes © 2020 by Brendan O'Callaghan.

Costigan Family History, recorded on two tapes © 1993 by Michael P. Costigan.

SONG REFERENCES

If you knew Susie, written by Buddy DeSylva and Joseph Meyer, published by Shapiro, Bernstein and Co., 1925.

Minnie the Moocher, written by Cab Calloway, Irving Mills and Clarence Gaskill, published by Brunswick, March 3, 1931.

Oh! Susanna, written by Stephen Foster, published in 1848.

The Charleston, composed by James P. Johnson for the Broadway musical 'Runnin' Wild', 1923.

GLOSSARY

Ancestral Healing: This involves healing your ancestors' unresolved issues, problems or trauma, using family knowledge, research or intuition. Ancestral Healing may lead to personal healing and transformation.

Ancestral Memory: Also referred to as Genetic Memory in psychology. It is a theory that memory may be present from birth that exists in the absence of sensory experience, and is incorporated into the genome over long spans of time. Hence, memories may be carried from one generation to another.

Angel Reading: A service provided by an angel reader, often using angel cards, to tap into angelic presence, to guide the recipient towards their best life situation. Readings may focus on a specific question or may be more open-ended, simply honing in on general aspects of life. They may also be effective in tuning into subconscious thoughts, emotions and visions that may serve as guidance.

Attraction (Law of): The belief that positive or negative thoughts attract similar experiences in people's lives.

Biocentrism: In a political and ecological sense, it is an ethical point of view that extends inherent value to all living things. It is an understanding of how the earth works, particularly as it relates to biodiversity, i.e. the variety and variability of life on earth.

Buddhism: A religion and philosophy that was founded by Siddhartha Gautama, known as 'the Buddha', the Enlightened One, more than 2,500 years ago, in India. It is estimated to have about 470 million followers worldwide. Its practice has historically been most prominent in East and Southeast Asia, but its influence is growing in the West. Many Buddhist ideas and philosophies overlap with those of other faiths. Adherents belief that spirits are reincarnated a number of times and live a series of lives on earth, before reaching enlightenment.

Cause and Effect (Law of): Every action has a reaction or consequence. This is summed up in the Christian lesson that "for whatever one sows, that will he also reap" (Galatians, 6:7-8). Thus, every act carries an effect, whether positive or negative. In Buddhist terms, this is known as Karma. Also see Karma.

Christianity: A religion that is monotheistic (ie. having a belief in one God), based on the life and teachings of Jesus of Nazareth. Its followers, known as Christians, believe that Jesus is the Christ, whose coming as the messiah was prophesied in the Hebrew Bible, called the Old Testament in

Christianity, and chronicled in the New Testament. Adherents believe that people live on earth once and that when they die there will be a process of judgement.

Clairaudience (clear-hearing): The ability to hear messages either audibly or in the mind, from the spirit realm.

Claircognizance: (clear-knowing): The ability to 'just know' information that comes spontaneously through ones intuition.

Clairsentience: (clear-feeling): The ability to feel strongly and sense the emotions and feelings of people, animals, spirits, and places.

Clairvoyance: (clear-seeing): The ability to see images or scenes, either manifested physically or in the mind, from the spirit realm.

Clairvoyant: A person who has the ability to see images or scenes, either manifested physically or in the mind, from the spirit realm.

Consciousness: A state of being aware and responsive. In spiritual terms, it is equated with spirit or the essence of life.

Déjà vu: In French, meaning 'already seen'. As a psychic experience, it is the overwhelming sense of familiarity with a person or place that should not be familiar.

Enlightenment: The state of being enlightened and achieving full awareness. In Buddhist terms, this is the realisation of Nirvana. Also see Nirvana.

Extra-Sensory: Sensing outside of the usual five senses: sight, hearing, smell, taste and touch. This may also be referred to as having a sixth sense, or a heightened intuition, where information is deduced without previous experience.

Extra-Sensory Perception (ESP): Perception (as in telepathy, clairvoyance, and precognition) that involves awareness of information about events that are extra-sensory, ie. external to the self and not gained through the five senses and not deducible from previous experience.

Hinduism: A religion that originated in India and has 1.25 billion followers, known as Hindus, in most Asian countries. Adherents believe that spirits are reincarnated a number of times and live a series of earth lives, before reaching enlightenment.

Hypnoanalysis: Based on Sigmund Freud's therapy, psychoanalysis, using hypnosis to relax a person sufficiently, to allow buried memories to be recalled and released, to facilitate deep emotional healing.

Hypnosis: A condition involving focused attention, reduced peripheral awareness and an enhanced capacity to respond to suggestion, whereby a person can be facilitated to recall previously forgotten memories and events.

Genetic Memory: See Ancestral Memory.

In Utero: In the womb, before birth.

Islam: A religion that is monotheistic (i.e. having a belief in one God) that teaches that there is only one God, Allah, and that Muhammad is a messenger of God. It has over 1.8 billion followers, known as Muslims. Adherents believe that people live once and that when they die there will be a process of judgement.

Judaism: A religious, cultural and legal tradition of the Jewish people. It is considered to be the expression of the covenant that God established with the Children of Israel. It has between 14.5 and 17.4 million followers, known as Jews. Adherents believe that people live once and that when they die there will be a process of judgement.

Karma: In Hinduism and Buddhism, the sum total of a person's actions in this and previous states of existence, viewed as deciding their fate in future existences. Also see Cause and Effect (Law of).

Meditation: The practice of a technique, such as mindfulness, visualisation, or focusing the mind on a particular object, thought or activity, such as the breath, with the purpose of training attention and awareness, to achieve a mentally clear and emotionally calm state of mind.

Medium: See Spirit Medium.

Mindfulness: The psychological process of purposefully bringing one's attention to experiences occurring in the present moment, without judgment, which one develops through the practice of meditation and through other forms of training.

Monotheistic: The belief that there is only one God.

Nirvana: In Buddhism, this is a transcendent state in which there is neither suffering, desire, nor a sense of self, where the subject is released from the effects of karma and the cycle of death and rebirth. It represents the final goal of Buddhism. Also see Enlightenment.

Past-Life Regression Therapy: See Regression.

Past Lives: The belief that a person's spirit has lived previous lives in other bodies. Also see Reincarnation.

Precognition: The knowledge of a future event or situation, especially through extra-sensory means.

Psychic: Relating to or denoting faculties or phenomena that are apparently inexplicable by natural laws, especially involving telepathy, clairaudience, claircognizance, clairsentience and clairvoyance.

Quantum Consciousness: Also known as Quantum Mind, a group of hypotheses proposing that classical mechanics cannot explain consciousness. It proffers that quantum mechanical phenomena may be an important part in the brain's function and may explain consciousness.

Quantum Mind: See Quantum Consciousness.

Quantum Physics: The physics that explains how everything works: The nature of the particles that make up matter and the forces with which they interact.

Rebirth: See Reincarnation.

Regression: Also known as Past-Life Regression Therapy. It refers to a technique, using a form of visualisation and hypnosis, which facilitates an individual going back through time to their previous lives, by accessing normally hidden memories in the subconscious mind.

Reincarnation: The religious or philosophical belief that the spirit of a living being begins an earth life in a different physical body after biological death. It is also referred to as rebirth or transmigration. The concept is central to the Buddhist and Hindu religions.

Samsara: In Sanskrit, meaning 'wandering' or 'world', pertaining to the cyclic nature of rebirth in the Hindu religion.

Sixth Sense: See Extra-Sensory.

Soulmate: A person with whom one has a feeling of deep or natural affinity. In spiritual terms, soulmates are two different souls that share a deep spiritual connection over many lifetimes.

Soul Twin: See Twin Souls.

Spirituality: A sense or belief that we each have a spirit that is eternal and that each spirit is connected to something bigger than ourselves, such as God or a Divine presence. It usually involves a search for meaning in life.

Spirit Guides: Beings from the spiritual realm who act as guides to a person living an earth life, particularly in the fulfilment of the person's plan that he or she devised before an earth life. Spirit Guides may offer support and guidance but only when given permission by the person they are guiding.

Spirit Medium: Also referred to as spiritual or spiritualist medium. A person who has fined-tuned his or her extra-sensory perceptions and can communicate with the spirit world.

Spiritual Healing: Healing channelled from the spiritual realm, from the highest level of light, through the healer's spirit and to the recipient of healing.

Spiritual Reading: A facility offered by a spirit medium who can relay information from the spirit world, from loved ones in spirit and from spirit guides, about past lives, present insights and possible future events.

Synchronicity (Law of): The simultaneous occurrence of events which appear significantly related but have no discernible causal connection.

Telepathy: The supposed communication of thoughts or ideas by means other than the known senses.

Transmigration: The movement of a soul into another body. Also see Reincarnation.

Twin souls: Also known as soul twins. In spiritual terms, two souls that are each half of the same soul, making up a complete soul.

Visualisation: Using ones imagination, usually imagining a beautiful scene or a colour to instil deep relaxation, to facilitate healing or personal exploration.

FURTHER WORKS BY LUCY COSTIGAN

BOOKS

Yvette's Transformation, Enlighten Publishing, Wexford, 2020.

Finding Meaning In Cosmic Order, Divine Plans, and Everyday Life, Enlighten Publishing, Wexford, 2020.

Conscious Moment: Finding Peace Amid the Din, Enlighten Publishing, Wexford, 2020.

The Last Day of Harry Clarke: Three Act Play (with Anthony Costigan and Theresa Cullen), Enlighten Publishing, Wexford, 2019.

Dark Beauty: Hidden Detail in Harry Clarke's Stained Glass (with Michael Cullen), Merrion Press, Dublin, 2019.

Understanding Suicide: Exploring the World of Pain within the Suicide Box (with Anthony E. Walsh), Currach Press, Dublin, 2015.

Winter Solstice: A Novel, Enlighten Publishing, Wexford, 2014.

Glenveagh Mystery: The Life, Work and Disappearance of Arthur Kingsley Porter, Merrion Press, Dublin, 2012.

Strangest Genius: The Stained Glass of Harry Clarke, The History Press, Dublin, 2010.

Bullying and Harassment in the Workplace, Columba Press, Dublin, 1997.

Irish Guide to Complementary and Alternative Therapies, Wolfhound Press, Dublin, 1996.

FILM DOCUMENTARIES

Journey Through Glass, Irishimages.org/film, (to be released in 2020): www.harryclarke.net.

A Revel in Blue: The Life and Work of Harry Clarke, 2010, (with Anthony Costigan, Theresa Cullen, Michael Cullen and Raymond J. McGovern): www.harryclarke.net.

ABOUT THE AUTHOR

Lucy Costigan is an Irish author. 'Strangest Genius: The Stained Glass of Harry Clarke', (with photographer Michael Cullen), was shortlisted for Best Irish-Published Book in 2010 by the Irish Book Awards, and for Book of the Decade by Dublin Book Festival in 2016. In 2012, Lucy's biography, 'Glenveagh Mystery' about the Harvard professor, Arthur Kingsley Porter, who mysteriously disappeared from Co. Donegal in 1933, became a national bestseller. Lucy's working life has been quite eclectic and includes careers in technical writing, counselling and social care. She holds Master's Degrees in Research and Equality Studies. Lucy lives in Wexford Town with her partner, Tony, and their border collie, Ivan.